ordinary joy

Finding Fresh Promise in Routine Moments

JOE CAMPEAU

Augsburg Books
MINNEAPOLIS

For Jim and Helen.
You were the first to show me love.
You were the first to show me Christ.

ORDINARY JOY
Find Fresh Promise in Routine Moments

Large-quantity purchases or custom editions of this book are available at a discount from the publisher. For more information, contact the sales department at Augsburg Fortress, Publishers, 1-800-328-4648, or write to: Sales Director, Augsburg Fortress, Publishers, Box 1209, Minneapolis, MN 55440-1209.

Descriptions of experiences in this book are factually based and reflect the opinions of the author. Some of the names and specific details of individuals have been changed to protect their privacy.

Unless otherwise indicated, Scripture is taken from the Holy Bible, New International Version ® , copyright © 1973, 1978, 1984 International Bible Society. Used by permission of Zondervan Publishing House. All rights reserved.

Scripture quotations marked NRSV are from the New Revised Standard Version Bible, copyright © 1989 by the Division of Christian Education of the National Council of the Churches of Christ in the USA. Used by permission.

Library of Congress Cataloging-in-Publication Data
Campeau, Joe, 1955-
  Ordinary joy : finding fresh promise in routine moments / by Joe Campeau.
    p. cm.
  Includes bibliographical references.
  ISBN 0-8066-5145-8 (pbk. : alk. paper)
  1. Christian life—Lutheran authors. 2. Bible. N.T. Gospels—Meditations. I. Title.
  BV4501.3.C3575 2005
  242—dc22   2005016182

Cover design by Diana Running; Cover photo © PhotoDisc/Getty Images. Used by permission.
Book design by Michelle L. N. Cook

The paper used in this publication meets the minimum requirements of American National Standard for Information Sciences—Permanence of Paper for Printed Library Materials, ANSI Z329.48-1984. ⊜ ™

Manufactured in the U.S.A.

09   08   07   06   05   1   2   3   4   5   6   7   8   9   10

Contents

Acknowledgments

This book has been a group effort. I am thankful for the many people who have been a part of my life, some of whose stories are included in these pages, who have pointed me consistently and gently to the presence of God in countless ordinary moments.

Lynne Rieck and Cindy Whetsel read the manuscript and suggested changes that made the work stronger. They both get extra credit for having endured the mangled grammar, suspect use of semicolons, and occasionally tortured language of the rough cut.

Like a fine jeweler, Marcia Broucek, with her editing skills, cleaned, cut, and polished until what was uneven became something that looked like I knew what I was doing. Her positive encouragement from the beginning eased my considerable anxiety.

The people of Christ Lutheran Church are an endless well of grace and joy, providing consistent support and constant encouragement. Their love touches me deeply. There is not another group of people for whom I would feel more privileged to serve.

And Barbie . . . you always knew, even when I wasn't sure. Thank you.

A Closer Look

"Look closer."

"I *am* looking closer," I said, frustration rising in my throat. "I've been staring at this bicycle now for two hours, and all I see is a bicycle."

"Then look closer," Rich urged.

I was taking photography lessons from my friend Rich who, in another time and place, had been a photojournalist. The key to taking interesting pictures, Rich explained, was in learning not to just look at an object, but to see it with fresh eyes, to recognize what is present but unnoticed. Rich gave me an assignment: Take thirty-six pictures of the same object. Each composition had to be different, not because of a change in surroundings but because it reflected a different point of view. Since I was a cycling enthusiast, I chose my bike.

The assignment seemed easy at first: Here's my bike from the front. This is my bike from the back, from the

---

side, here's a view from the top . . . now what? This was impossible. I squeezed off about ten frames, and I was stuck. There was nothing left to see, no pictures left to take.

"Look closer."

I threw up my arms to make sure Rich knew how unreasonable he was being, again leaned in toward the bike, and wondered what he could see that I was missing. "It's easy for you," I grumbled. "You've trained your eyes to recognize beauty. All I see are a few metal tubes and a couple of wheels." That's when I noticed the graphic pattern the spokes made as they flared out from the wheel hub, intersecting each other in a pattern called "lacing." I grabbed my camera and moved in tight for a close-up. Glancing toward the handlebars, I realized how gracefully the brake cables curved and how interesting they were from this angle. Soon I could see how bits of dirt and grease clung to the chain, creating miniature mountain ranges.

Rich taught me a fundamental principle of photography that day: Look closer. If you want to see beauty, learn to view ordinary things in new ways.

Applying the same principle to life reveals the potential for joy. We live most of life firmly in the grip of the ordinary. The beginning of most days echoes the start of the day before. The alarm pierces the best sleep of the night, and as usual, you're late before the day has even begun. The kids are fighting an explosive battle over something profoundly unimportant. The bills lie scattered across the desk waiting to be paid from a checkbook whose financial health was terminal a week ago. Your day gifts you with clogging traffic, a sniping boss, and a demanding customer. Back home again, your spouse is snapping, the dog is whining, the car is failing, and dinner is on the run so everyone can make his or her evening commitments. A sigh escapes your lips; something like sadness fogs your heart. The thought crosses your mind: "Where's the happiness in a day like this? Shouldn't life be something more?" Just as quickly, you regret the question. You know you have it pretty good. Still . . .

Ordinary life. Commonplace days. The daily drone of the routine. If your tomorrows look suspiciously like your yesterdays, you know how difficult it can be to discover—and hold onto—a durable joy.

Could our resistance to the ordinary be why, as a culture, we're so fascinated by celebrities? Browse the magazine racks. Check out the tabloid news shows. We seem to have an insatiable appetite for information on the rich, the famous, the beautiful. From the latest exploits of movie stars, to the off-court behavior of athletic marvels, to any given rock star's most recent metamorphosis, our nation's interest in the latest celebrity adventure never fades. Tragic or heroic, they represent life beyond the confines of the ordinary. Their lives move beyond the boundaries hemming in the rest of us. They seem bigger, stronger, different, uncommon, never dull, and always more able than us regular folks. They reach higher and go farther. Their lives titillate; their exploits become movies of the week; their strengths and weaknesses are magnified by our own curiosity. They do the things we can never do; they rack up the accomplishments of which we can only dream. Their days are unlike the dull routines that fill our own.

Reality television is the latest twist on this endless fascination. Producers select ordinary people to participate in extraordinary adventures, resulting in a few minutes of fame and a spot on a late night talk show where they are ordinary no more. As a culture, we're not sure whether we prefer to cheer them on because they started out like us, or jeer them because watching them fail lifts our own sense of self-worth.

There is something, well . . . ordinary . . . about being ordinary. The routine becomes a drag. Any recognition that comes is fleeting at best. The sun rises and sets on the same problems each day. Sometimes it seems our lives should be graded with a "C," that dreaded mark that always meant just average—not bad but no distinction either. We'd like our lives to look like a Monet watercolor, but more often it resembles a velvet Elvis.

Spiritual life fares little better. Do you find yourself wishing your faith could feel more vibrant, your ministry more significant when, in fact, words such as fatigue or resentment might be more descriptive? The joy can drain away. One more batch of cookies for the Hospitality Committee. Yet another evening of filling a chair at a meeting. An additional voice in the choir. Life and ministry sometimes taste more of duty than joy. Not exactly soul stirring when compared with the stories in the Bible.

The Bible often appears to be a book of heroes. It is filled with epic stories about larger-than-life people who, through God's strength, did spectacular things. They were flawed characters, to be sure. They made mistakes, their faith weakened on occasion, they may have been confused now and then. Still, they are the giants of Scripture. You know who they are: Moses, Mary, Peter, Paul . . . they are the Bible's headliners. Their stories tower above those around them. And where does that leave you and me?

I don't know about you, but by comparison I'm pretty ordinary. Most days I don't feel much like a Moses. No one would mistake me for Peter, except perhaps in his weaker moments. Paul? Not a chance. These titans of faith were the stars of the show. Most days I feel more like a walk-on, a bit player who forgets his lines on opening night. They hit the ball into the upper decks; I strike out on the third pitch. They ran the race and finished with a powerful stride; I sometimes feel like dropping out altogether.

Any of this sound familiar?

The Bible, however, is also full of average people. Men and women, sometimes nameless, whose stories we rarely remember and seldom mention. Their lives are the MUZAK of Scripture. Ordinary people. Like me, like you. Everyday individuals in the midst of usual circumstances whose lives carried the same conflicts, whose days contained the same headaches, whose existence held the same boredom, frustrations, and challenges as ours. They were neither flamboyant, exceptional, nor competitors for spiritual gold medals. But they had something in common other than the low billing they share in Scripture's cast of characters: They each caught the scent of joy in the midst of the ordinary. When they met Jesus, they discovered new depth in their common lives, fresh promise in routine moments.

Need some examples? There was a father, desperate to get help for his son, who came looking for Jesus (Mark 9). The Gospels tell of an anonymous woman who anointed Jesus' feet simply out of devoted love (Luke 7). A boy with nothing to offer but a bit of bread and a couple fish suddenly found himself in the middle of a miracle (John 6). And what of the nameless man Jesus healed? When asked to give an account of what happened, the man could only stammer, "Look, I couldn't see before and now I can. Jesus made the difference, and that's all I can say for sure" (John 9).

When we examine the stories of these biblical "extras," something becomes clear: Joy resides less in the extraordinary things of life and more in recognizing God in the midst of the ordinary. The great good news of following Jesus is not that he promises life will be one continuous spiritual high from which the faithful never descend. There is no promise that our lives and our faith will be charted from one spike to the next on the spirituality index. If that were the curve on which my faith life were to be graded, my spirit would grow weary before I ever reached midterms. Still, isn't that the way we self-grade our lives? Do we expect that, because we are people of faith, our spiritual experience should somehow be more consistently a grand adventure? Are we disappointed, do we feel as if something is wrong with our faith life, if it isn't more dynamic?

Here's the reality: My life is not one of greatness or memorable achievements. Yours probably isn't either. My life has more to do with parenting challenges than with great deeds of faith. Holding down a job while juggling family commitments, community activities, and the other endless, demanding details of life is more a part of my day than participating in miracles. I suspect your life is pretty much like mine.

The first key to finding uncommon joy at the center of common life is to recognize God in the middle of it. It involves training our spirit to discover God on ordinary days, working grace in ordinary ways. Nestled between arguments with the boss and a car that won't start is the persistent presence of God. In the course of a day filled with more demands than hours in which to satisfy them, as a part of our daily routine, in the eye of our daily storms, God whispers our name. Recognizing God in the midst of the mundane enables us to discover divinity in dullness, harvest hope from humdrum. A common day becomes a holy one. The daily routine turns out to be the very place we meet God. The normal becomes a novel opportunity for sacred adventure. Identifying God in the middle of our most usual, unspectacular living transforms our days into sacramental moments. The surprising joy of faith is discovering how close God has always been.

The second key to finding ordinary joy is to recognize the ways in which the simplest areas of life can also be the most profound arenas for serving God. It begins when we acknowledge that life is not something owned, but offered. The strength of God's kingdom, the vitality of Christ's church, the sharing of a message of startling love—it all happens through uncertain, sometimes confused, often unspoken and unspectacular people playing unsuspecting roles in God's plan. People like you. People like Becky.

Jesus used Becky's arms to wrap Madeline in his embrace. Madeline was an old woman, interred by her frail health behind the walls of her apartment. Her companions were the nurses who came to care for her an hour each day, and her social life consisted of visits to her doctor. Most of Madeline's friends were dead; her husband was buried; one son, too, had died before her. A daughter lived the better part of two states away. What friends Madeline had left were busy with their own lives, intending to visit but never quite arriving at her door.

One day Becky, with her daughter, Ariel, stopped by my office and asked if there were anyone I knew who could use a visit. Becky was a working mom with an active six-year-old. Her husband was frequently gone on business for extended periods of time, leaving her to handle much of the parenting and household responsibilities on her own. But visiting was something Becky wanted to do, so I suggested she stop by and see Madeline.

Becky and Ariel began visiting regularly. They would stop in for a few minutes now and then, bringing a smile with them, talking about nothing of great importance, and giving Madeline someone for whom she could crochet a gift. In a child's scrawl Ariel would send thank-you notes to Madeline, and Becky would hug an old woman for whom hugs had become a thing forgotten.

A busy mother and her young daughter—they do not qualify as front-page material. They earned no headlines, attracted no spotlight. They did nothing remarkable . . . except provide an everyday friendship in an extraordinary way to a woman for whom the darkness was creeping close. Just before Madeline died, she extracted a promise from me. Her funeral was to be strictly private except for three people: her daughter, Becky, and Ariel.

There are many days when we are not called to be heroes. There are circumstances that demand nothing more than that we remain faithful. There are moments, easily missed and quickly gone, when we have the opportunity not for great deeds of faith requiring supreme sacrifices, but for simple acts of love and service. An encouraging word to a child. A hopeful smile. A gentle response in the midst of a harsh world. A well-timed phone call. A pat on the back. A cup of coffee. These are the small miracles of love that press the touch of Jesus into people's lives.

Life's joy reveals itself not only as we encounter a Savior who weaves himself into the fabric of routine living, but as we act on his invitation to rediscover the significance of serving him in ordinary ways. The most inconsequential detail of a servant life carries with it all the power of God's grace, for Jesus transforms the ordinary things we do into something more.

Could you use some joy? Does the concert of the routine play on in your life, dulling its meaning and emptying its delight?

"Look closer," my friend reminded me. That's pretty good advice. Rather than seeing the ordinary as something to be avoided or a source of discontent, look closer. Peer deeper. Joy arrives when you discover God's fingerprints on the surface of each day.

part one

Discovering God
on Ordinary Days

chapter one

Jesus Kisses Us

Jesus said, "You believe because I told you I saw you under the fig tree. You shall see greater things than that." (John 1:50)

Days of gray drizzle had finally given way to brilliant spring sunlight. The road was lined with puddles from the previous rains, but the sun was finally breaking through! Somehow the spirit lifts a bit and the world sparkles more when the sun returns after an extended absence. My son Sam, about five years old at the time, and I were together in the car going about our normal Saturday errands when he began talking about the newly shining sun.

"You know, Dad, when the sun is warm on your head? Well, that's just like Jesus kissing you. Jesus is kissing you when the sun is shining on your head. And, Dad, you can't wipe his kiss off."

Back then Sam and I played a game together each night. I would kiss him, and he would pretend to wipe it away. When I tucked him into bed, he would allow one kiss and no more. If I left the room and moments later snuck back in to steal another kiss, he would be prepared. If I persisted in trying to get a second kiss, he even had an arrangement with his mother to escort me from the room. He would "cement" in place with a few hand motions the kisses from my wife, Barbie, but mine he would wipe off. I was not allowed to try and keep Sam from wiping off the kiss I had just given him. Our game made us laugh together.

As we made our way through this particular Saturday's routine, however, Sam had other things on his mind. "Dad," he explained, "you can't ever wipe off Jesus' kiss. It just stays."

At such a tender age Sam understood what so many of us miss, what we so easily forget: God is continually looking for ways to kiss us. In fact, God showers us with kisses each day. God's world teems with the evidence of our Creator's passion. But like a gardener who no longer notices the beauty of the flowers for which she cares, we tend to see only the mundane without noticing any of the miraculousness it contains. Our problem lies not in an inactive God but in our inability to recognize the signs of our Creator's grace.

One day my secretary called me, desperate for a translation. She did not need a translation from Greek to English, or a technical phrase into common language. She needed to decode hieroglyphics into legible handwriting. My scrawl is not the easiest to read, and she does an admirable job deciphering what sometimes even I am unable to identify. But occasionally the word hides so effectively in the erratic scratching that she just can't determine what it is. Then she calls me for a translation.

The word in question that day was "grace."

"Oh," she said, "it's 'grace.' I guess I just don't know grace when I see it."

She's not alone. In a world of budgets, megabyte computers, and humming technology, our imaginations become infertile, and we often fail to recognize grace. We become numb to the frequency with which God kisses us. The Savior can make himself known, but all we see is what we have always seen. What we expect to see. The Divine can sing us a love song, but all we hear is the background noise.

Nathaniel had the same problem. He may have been a disciple, but he is rarely mentioned in the Gospels. Nor did he get off to a very good start. There he was, sitting under a fig tree thinking about the kinds of things we all do when we have a few minutes alone, when his brother Philip rushed up, gulping between breaths, "We've found the Messiah! He's from Nazareth."

Nathaniel was not impressed. He knew Nazareth and what to expect from such a place. The only thing for which Nazareth was known was that the foreign occupation force garrisoned there. How could the Messiah come from a backwater, nondescript place like Nazareth?

When Philip invited Nathaniel to come meet Jesus, all Nathaniel could see was a carpenter. The Messiah stood right in front of him, and Nathaniel didn't recognize him. This Jesus was too ordinary for Nathaniel's expectations, too plain. It wasn't until this common man from a common town spoke with uncommon insight into Nathaniel's heart that Nathaniel realized in whose company he was. It was all Nathaniel needed. "Rabbi," he said, "you are the Son of God."

Philip brought Nathaniel to Jesus, and Nathaniel almost turned away. Jesus came to me in the living room of a woman named Hannah, and I almost missed him, too. Hannah was an older, shut-in member of my congregation, and it was my turn to visit her and bring communion. That day I went out of duty, not joy.

The slate-gray skies of a November day were as damp and dull as my spirit. It was the end of a singularly bad week, coming on the heels of many other weeks just like it. I wanted to go home. I wanted to stare into space. I wanted to do almost anything other than what I was about to do. The rain-soaked day cast a constant drizzle that saturated any of my remaining enthusiasm.

I knocked on the door. Hannah called out for me to come in, and I entered her cramped, drab living room. We visited for a bit, and I wondered how long I had to stay before I could make an exit without appearing rude. Finally, I thought I saw my opening. Moving to the edge of the chair, I was ready to make a break for the door with a hasty apology and a promise to return—and then Hannah asked if she could read something to me.

I sagged back into the chair.

"Of course," I replied with a tone far more pleasant than my attitude.

Hannah picked up her Bible and read from the first chapter of Ephesians. ". . . [God] chose us in Christ before the foundation of the world to be holy and blameless before him in love. He destined us for adoption as his children through Jesus Christ . . ." (Ephesians 1:4-5 NRSV). As she read, a smile crept across her ancient mouth. This old woman could barely contain her excitement at the thought that, at her age, she was still a child. And not just a child, but a child of the most high God.

She closed her Bible and, with it, her eyes. When she opened them, she looked directly at me. "I just wanted to share that with you. I found it the other day. Maybe you needed to hear that like I did. It sounds pretty good, doesn't it?"

Hannah could not know the extent of what she did for me. There I was, the pastor who was supposed to be ministering to her needs and, without knowing it, she was ministering to mine. The professional caregiver was being given a bit of water for a heart of dust. I left renewed. Restored. Remade. But more than that, Jesus had come to find me in the form of a woman who could barely make out the words she was reading. As he did for Nathaniel, Jesus came at a time I did not expect, in a place I was not prepared to meet him, through a person I did not think likely, in a way I did not anticipate. For a moment, on a gray November day, the Son kissed me.

Just as it surprised Nathaniel to discover that a common man from a run-of-the-mill town could be the Savior, common experiences can reacquaint us with our uncommon God. We discover joy not by stumbling across something unexpectedly good, but by recognizing the goodness of all that is usual in life. Everything—no matter how small, common, or unremarkable, no matter how many times we've seen it or how often we've experienced it—can offer a glimpse of grace, a warm kiss from the One who made us. Even the most ordinary events can carry a divine caress when we are open to sensing their uniqueness.

To live life in the presence of Jesus is to perceive things not seen before. If we open our eyes, if we look closely, there is God kissing us in each moment.

When was the last time you noticed an individual petal on a single flower, uncurling to meet the sun? At that particular moment in that specific landscape, did you recall the One who painted it?

Have you recently entered your child's room as she slept, to watch the regular in and out of her breathing? As you gently reached to brush back her hair, perhaps your own breath came a little faster and your pulse quickened at the miracle who terrorized you today but now sleeps secure in your care.

Put your finger to your wrist right now. (Go ahead, put the book down; I'll wait for you.) There . . . did you feel the pulse? You live one surge of blood at a time. Each time you feel the blood rush beneath your fingertips, it is another gifted moment. Another message that the One who created you is the One who remembers you and graces you with goodness moment by moment, morning by morning.

Tomorrow after the alarm goes off, the shower will be standing by, the coffee will need brewing, and the daily schedule will already be frowning at your inability to meet its demands. But wait. Don't get up yet. Spend a moment and notice the wind blowing the curtains into your room with its freshening breath. Breathe in the scent of the rain as it restores the dry earth. Look at the clouds beginning to break revealing the blue sky that was always behind them. Listen to the singing birds riding the tree limbs that are doing the dance of creation.

Sometimes we're conscious of God's miracles, and we recognize them all around us, like the warm sun on our head after a run of overcast days. Other times we can be remarkably oblivious to God's presence as we go about our lives. We can become so used to God's kiss that we grow inattentive to it. I now live in Southern California where the sun always shines, and there are times when I barely pay attention to it. But the ease with which I let the sun go unnoticed does not make it refuse to shine. Nor does a cavalier attitude toward our Creator's grace cause God to stop kissing us. The sun will shine tomorrow, and the Son will kiss us once again.

Know what the best part is? Sam does. It can never be wiped away.

Some Things to Think About

1. Think about the past twenty-four hours. When have you felt God's kiss? If nothing comes to mind, look closer, consider the small signs.

2. The author uses his son's bedtime kiss as a metaphor for God's presence and grace in our lives. What other metaphors might you use to describe God's presence and grace in your life?

3. What are some things that make it difficult for you, like Nathaniel, to recognize the Jesus who is right in front of you?

4. What might you do differently tomorrow when you wake up to be more aware of God's presence? How might you carry that attitude with you through your day?

5. Name a time when you needed someone's caring. What did you *think* you needed? What did you actually receive?

6. What might you do in the next twenty-four hours to be God's kiss for someone else?

chapter two

Hurry-Up Holiness

... Jesus asked [the blind man], "Do you see anything?" He looked up and said, "I see people; they look like trees walking around." Once more Jesus put his hands on the man's eyes. Then his eyes were opened, his sight was restored, and he saw everything clearly. (Mark 8:23-25)

When today's obligations steal tomorrow's hopes, joy is the first casualty. One of the hazards of ordinary life is how slowly it meets our expectations. Long-held goals wilt under the glare of daily realities. Plans once made, like shimmering desert pools, never quite materialize. What we set out to achieve has yet to be accomplished. Paths are taken, choices are made, and dreams deferred. We find ourselves caught at the midpoint between what we were and what we had hoped to become. Instead of celebrating the life we live, we live with a nagging dissatisfaction over the life we don't have, spending our days pursuing a joy that is maddeningly elusive.

We're in a hurry; life runs at full throttle. Anything that causes delay is a frustration. Ordinary living can seem dull because the pace of our dreams outstrips the ability of our experiences to fulfill them.

It reminds me of my microwave. While the days are not far removed when an oven and a stovetop ruled the kitchen, that is no longer true. The microwave has overthrown them and established itself as the dominant appliance, and the proudest ones of all are those with the highest power. They are the ovens able to finish their cooking job in the shortest amount of time.

Few American households are without some kind of microwave. Many hotels include them in their furnishings. Restaurants use them. Offices keep them handy. And no wonder; they fit so well into our typical high-speed lifestyle. No need to wait for water to heat so the vegetables can cook; just zap them in the micro. Want the leftovers warm? No problem: nuke 'em. Running behind? There's still time for dinner when frozen entrees are can be prepared in minutes with the speed of a microwave. Punch in the time, pull out the finished product, and all is ready to eat and run. We are an instant people with eighteen-second attention spans, so the sociologists tell us—if we even pay attention long enough to hear the message. Instant answers are as popular as instant soup. We are not inclined to take the long view.

What if faith worked like microwaves? Pop yourself into a relationship with Jesus, turn the Spirit on high, and in the blink of an eye your life is changed. No more selfishness. No more unjustified anger. No more embarrassing character flaws. Holiness in nothing flat for those without the time to wait. Immediate transformation instead of painful growth. This may be great for microwaves, but when the Apostle Paul tells us, "We . . . are being transformed into his likeness . . ." (2 Corinthians 3:18), that's not quite what he had in mind.

When we enter a relationship with Jesus, we know instinctively that it will change us. The Scriptures point that out. The evidence is clear from the lives of others who have experienced Christ's transforming love. We've heard it in their testimonies; we've read it in their books. When I look at the lives not just of Mother Teresa and

Billy Graham but of people such as Bob down the street, a Christian I know and admire, that's the way I'd like to be. But that's not the way I am.

What is true in life is true in spirit: We're in a spiritual hurry.

I wonder why the Spirit doesn't change me more quickly. How is it I can aspire to such a life of faith and yet fall so dramatically short? The truth is, when I go back and read my old journals, I realize I'm still struggling with the same sins that plagued me five years ago. The same temptations, the same habits, the same proclivities remain a part of me. I continue to struggle with investing my ministry in people's responses rather than in faithfulness to God. Impatience still reigns within me. An undisciplined prayer life still haunts my days. An uncanny ability to overlook the needs of an individual still commands my actions. So it was, so it is, so it will be? What's going on here? I'm left wondering why my faith is still so underdeveloped, why the Spirit's working doesn't seem to transform me with the speed I thought it would. In the sanctification kitchen, I'm still cooking on a wood stove. Sound familiar?

It hurts to be caught at the midpoint, between what life promises and what reality delivers, between who we are and what God intends us to be. An expectation of instantaneous and sweeping change can leave a feeling of emptiness, disappointment, and guilt when it does not occur in the allotted time.

A quick scan of the Gospels might leave the impression that instant transformation was the order of the day. People were healed immediately. Lives were transformed in the blink of an eye. In the span of four short verses, Jesus invited himself to dinner, which prompted Zaccheaus to cash in a profitable business and give his ill-gotten gain back to those he cheated. A Samaritan woman had a single conversation with Jesus and proceeded to evangelize a large portion of her town. A bloodthirsty Saul saw a blinding light and became Paul. It would seem in the compressed world of the Scriptures that much of what Jesus accomplished in people's lives happened with an instantaneous touch.

But not always . . . not in one particular case. Mark introduces us to a blind man at Bethsaida (Mark 8:22-25). What began for him with moist fingertips pressed against useless eyes would end in sight. But not immediately. The eyes that once served only to swallow light into endless night would see the outrageous colors of sunset, clouds caressing a mountaintop, and the gentle face of the One whose hands had removed the darkness. But not before the man saw what seemed to be "people like trees, walking." After Jesus' first touch, the man's vision remained blurred and indistinct. It took a second touch.

The truth is, spiritual growth can be painfully slow. But consider the alternative.

We have a tree in our front yard, and every time I walk by, I wish it weren't there. The reason? It grows too quickly. Oh, I know why it was planted. We live in a planned community, and the developers, in their wisdom, put in fast-growing trees to provide shade for their new neighborhood. They wanted their new community to look well-established and mature overnight. So they chose a tree that, like Jack's beanstalk, grows so quickly, each morning it reaches new heights.

I don't know anyone who actually enjoys having one of those trees in their yard. Its wild, erratic limbs grow so rapidly, every year it must be trimmed completely back to the trunk, leaving nothing but a branchless stump. In the summer its rate of growth is such that interior leaves can't get enough light. They yellow and drop and wait to be raked up at the end of every week. It's called a Fruitless Mulberry, and, though I'm no arborist, I think I can guess why. Its growth is so fast, so sudden, fruit-bearing is an impossibility.

Therein lies the problem. Growth that should be continually occurring over an expanse of years is compressed into a single month. The results aren't always pleasant, and maturity becomes more a facade than a reality. That's also the danger in hurry-up holiness. We try to have the look of growth about us by attempting to change ourselves overnight. The result? Discouragement. Dissatisfaction. Another reason for our spiritual lives to seem ordinary and joyless.

Take another look at the blind man's story. It may have taken a second touch to restore the man's sight, but what mattered was not the number of touches required, but who was doing the touching. We, too, need Jesus to touch us, not just once, but again and again. Sometimes we get confused and think that the growth of faith and the maturing of trust is solely our responsibility. We think that we are the ones who must do the work, that holiness comes only after sweating through spiritual aerobics and hefting spiritual weights.

Jesus is the One who transforms, whose touch first brings light into darkness, and then restores focus to what has become fuzzy. The measurement is never on how transformed we believe ourselves to be, but on how gracious God is, and if, on occasion, we are conscious of some small success, some tiny change, for that we can only be thankful.

Not long ago my wife, Barbie, and I spent a day driving up the central California coast from San Louis Obispo to Big Sur. Our trip began under a heavy blanket of fog, which is not unusual for that stretch of road. The cool waters of the Pacific mix with warm summer air, and the result is a deep marine layer. It is one of the most scenic drives in the nation, but not most mornings.

Driving through a thick shroud of mist, headlights on, I could sense that there was something grand about the place, but it lay just beyond the ability of my senses to detect it. Somewhere a gull cried. The road, like an over-permed strand of hair twisted its way into the murky distance. For a fraction of a moment, I could almost make out a portion of the headlands rearing their majestic peaks, or a glimpse of the craggy coast, but then it was gone, covered again by the fog. The heart and soul of the place was there, waiting to be discovered, hiding itself behind a gray curtain, yet just out of sight.

But on occasion, if only for a moment, it revealed itself. And then I knew; this place was big. Bigger than me. Bigger than I had imagined. Bigger than the pictures I'd seen of it. As the day wore on and the clouds lifted, I could finally see all its beauty, the majesty of which I had caught only glimpses earlier. It was a gradual, day-long revelation. Perhaps that's what made it so remarkable.

We live our lives in the firm clasp of God's gracious embrace, but we may at times feel as if we must grope our way through life, wondering why this pain has come to us, why we have to struggle to capture a sense of God's nearness, why the things we most wish God would change within us seem to cling so fiercely, and whether God has left the building. But it turns out that even in those moments, when life's murkiest clouds swirl around us making it difficult to see what life and faith are all about, still we remain in the presence of Majesty.

The steady, sometimes tedious plodding of life, contrary to being where we most experience God's absence, is in fact the very location of God's presence. Jesus meets us there to touch our eyes as many times as it takes, astonishing us with hope and filling our ordinary days with meaning. God is working within us even if it takes time, even if, at the moment, nothing much seems to be happening.

That's the difference, I suppose, between the way a microwave works and the way a sculptor creates. Ryan is a member of my congregation and an artist. One of the sculptures he created is something I fondly call "Metal Jesus." At one point Ryan spent considerable time foraging in all manner of unexpected places for what the rest of us would consider junk. Pieces of scrap metal. Discarded springs. Worthless objects all, thrown away and forgotten. Then, through careful, time-consuming effort, he formed all of that trash into a sculpture of

Jesus hanging on the cross. It is perhaps the most moving sculpture of Jesus I have ever seen. Ryan has made something ugly into something valuable, welded broken things together to create a stunning work of stark beauty formed in the shape of the Savior.

Just so, each of us is a work in progress, a masterpiece being painstakingly created by the divine Sculptor from the damaged and discarded scraps of our lives. Each new bit of brokenness restored, each imperceptible fleck of hope welded to our spirit is a cause for joy. Though we may not perceive progress, the Sculptor already sees within us the creation we will become. Our ordinary days are, in fact, the tools of the Artist.

Our transformation begins as Christ gives us the light of grace by which we finally see ourselves clearly for who we are. He peels away all the rationalizations and self-justifications we use as a way of dealing with our guilt. Then he moves us to confession where we are able to drop our list of excuses. Finally, he brings us healing that frees us from the grip of our own agenda and releases us to live in obedience to his. Rarely does this transformation begin with obvious change or dramatic intervention. Sometimes it begins simply with grace enough to endure the present moment and a desire for what Christ intends to do in us in the future.

When we know who is at work, we can take the risk of change. When we remember the relationship between the Sculptor and the sculpture, we are free to let Christ shape us as he will with whatever process he chooses. God's grace will continue, the transforming work will continue . . . right up to the gates of heaven.

Until then, change takes time. A statue is sculpted one tap at a time. A gourmet meal never comes from a microwave. Flowers display their beauty only gradually. Healing is a process. Twenty-twenty vision does not necessarily return with the first touch.

The key to ordinary joy is finding it *in* the journey, not simply upon arrival.

Some Things to Think About

1. What parts of your day feel most hurried? What are some of the "casualties" of your busy schedule?

2. Think of someone you know who has made a significant change in their life. How long did it take? How long did it take before you noticed the change?

3. Think of a time when you felt that nothing was happening, but when you look back on it, something in fact was changing. What does that suggest to you about how God works?

4. What kind of circumstances tend to cloud your sight or obscure joy in your life? What would Jesus' healing for you look like?

5. Paul tells us that we are being transformed into Christ's likeness. What does that look like for you?

6. What do you wish could be changed within you? How long have you been working on, or hoping for, this change? What signs of progress do you see? How do you feel about the time it is taking? How could you imagine finding joy *in* the process?

chapter three

When the Giver
Is the Gift

Jesus asked, "Were not all ten cleansed? Where
are the other nine? Was no one found to return
and give praise to God except this foreigner?"
Then he said to him, "Rise and go; your faith has
made you well." (Luke 17:17-19)

Mounds of discarded wrapping paper towered around
us as Barbie and I neared the end of the wedding gifts. A
few friends and some family, who had waited patiently
for us to return from our honeymoon, joined us as we
opened our presents. One of Barbie's sisters sat nearby
meticulously recording the names attached to each gift
so we could send a note of appreciation.

Barbie reached for the next gift, handed the card to
me, and pulled the wrapping from a beautiful plaque.
Another beautiful plaque. It would go well with the
fourteen other beautiful plaques at our feet. There
must have been a special on wedding plaques the year
we were married for we received at least one copy of
every conceivable inspirational saying, calligraphied
on paper, painted on plaster, carved in wood. Unfortu-
nately, none of them could produce toast, which was
what we really needed.

I opened the card to discover that this particular plaque was a gift from Larry and Carol. Despite the abundance of our sudden plaque collection, I realized Larry and Carol had taken time to pick something they hoped would be meaningful. We had been on their minds as they journeyed out into a Minnesota February to select a gift that would support our new life together and reflect their care for us.

There was just one problem. Who were Larry and Carol? I leaned over to Barbie. "Do you know these people?"

"Not a clue. I thought you knew them."

"Never heard of them," I said.

We passed the card and gift around the room, hoping someone might identify the giver. Surely somebody would recognize the handwriting. Maybe they were friends of an uncle or aunt, a shirt-tail relative only a grandmother would know. No luck. Despite our best efforts, Larry and Carol remained a mystery. We had their gift, but we had no one to thank.

Twenty-five years later, I still don't know who they are or why they shared that plaque with us. But Larry and Carol's simple gift, in some ways barely distinguishable from the others surrounding it, carried a hidden message. With no one to whom we could be grateful, their gift continues to remind me that life reaches a richer potential when we know whom to thank.

We live in a world of gifts. Every breath draws grace into our soul. A solitary cloud skitters across an insistently blue sky, whispering the wonder of a Creator bent on sharing his handiwork with us. A twinkle in the eye of one who claims us as a friend, the quick "I love you" taken along when we leave for work, a sleepy "goodnight" from a child resting peacefully in our care . . . gifts, every last one of them. Common. Ordinary. They pile up in our lives with such frequency, one stacked upon another, that we may see them as little more than just another plaque.

The problem is one of focus. Most drug stores carry racks of reading glasses with varying magnifications. Sometimes, when my children are with me, I'll find the most outlandish frame, perch it on the end of my nose, and go looking up and down the aisles for one of them. Tapping them on the back, I'll wait for them to turn around as I ask, "What do you think? Is it *me?*" They used to laugh, but lately they just act embarrassed. The longer it takes to find them though, the more likely my little antic will give me a headache. The reason is simple: The focus is wrong. The lenses blur my vision, warp my view of what surrounds me, and tire my eyes. Poor focus will do that.

When dissatisfaction with ordinary living seeps into our days, chances are we have lost focus. Hiking through a forest dense with blessings and lush with mercy, we can fail to perceive the value of the commonplace. We lose sight of the gifts we have and focus our attention on those we lack. Life becomes a pursuit of that which is missing instead of a celebration of what we have received, distorting gladness until it is barely identifiable.

Recognizing the extraordinary nature of life's most common gifts paints the brushstrokes of joy across the muted colors of daily reality. But there is more. Moving beyond tallying the gifts to encountering the Giver colors our lives with joy's deepest hues.

Without a giver, a gift is simply another acquisition. The best gifts are those that come with the giver's heart attached so that in unwrapping the gift, we unwrap the love of the one who provided it. The nature of God's love is that all God's gifts come with God attached. Those gifts stretch beyond our understanding and link us to this God who inhabits the most common corners of life and fills them with deepest blessings.

Knowing whom to thank opens a door to ordinary joy.

This was true for ten men whom Jesus healed, and it is true for us. Luke provides an insight into gratitude when he relates the experience of these ten men with leprosy who came looking for him. More serious than the illness that ravaged their skin were the social consequences that devastated their lives. Their sickness made them ritually unclean. It disqualified them from worshiping in the synagogue or undertaking the practices their faith required. It left them unfit for human contact lest their ragged skin touch another person and render that person unclean as well. These men were not just victims of a numbing, degenerative disease, they were outcasts. Unwelcome. Pariahs among their people, they were untouchable to their family and friends.

When these men approached Jesus, they came looking for the one thing life had taught them they should least expect to receive: mercy. They came in hope of the very thing they would least likely find. They did not ask for a miracle. They did not request a healing. They were not awaiting the spectacular. All they wanted was mercy. A little kindness would be a sufficient gift. And Jesus gave it.

A disease as efficient at devastating human relationships as it was at destroying human tissue could not restrain Jesus. Ten men called out for compassion, and Jesus provided it, along with a bonus gift of fresh skin and restored health. A reason for thanks? Apparently not for nine out of the ten.

Ten were healed, but only one returned in gratitude. Ten received a gift, yet only one knew whom to thank. Jesus seemed a little disappointed with the whole situation. Can you hear the hurt in his voice?

"Where are the other nine? Didn't I heal ten? Where are the rest?"

This is not a portrait of a pouting Jesus, spitefully refusing to give another gift until someone showed a little gratitude. Jesus was concerned with something deeper.

Of interest to Jesus was what took place in the heart of one who thanked him. The lone leper to return was the only one to hear Jesus' final blessing, "Your faith has made you well." Apart from the physical healing the ten men received, this man alone connected the gift of healing to the value of knowing the Healer. More important than the gift of restored health was his encounter with the One who gave it.

The same holds true for us. More significant than the blessings we count is the One who bestows them. Our hearts grow a little softer, our spirits a little less wooden, our amazement at the giftedness of life a little more profound when we know whom to thank. There is a difference between being caught up in the gift and being caught up in the Giver. If we tie our gratitude too closely to the tangible gift, like the nine lepers, we'll miss the Giver.

We will never fully realize how close we are to the source of our life, to the well-spring of our healing, to the fulfillment of our desires until we take time out to praise the God who provides it all. When we sharpen our focus on the Giver, we are better able to recognize the gifts boiling up all around us. Then, the most commonplace gift becomes a treasure, and ordinary joy begins to sparkle.

Who knows, maybe Larry and Carol are reading this chapter. If so, there is something I need to say: Thank you. I know the gift you gave us was a plaque like so many others we received, but it has become something more. It serves as a reminder of the One who gives and gives and holds nothing back.

It is good to know whom to thank.

Some Things to Think About

1. Have you ever received a gift without knowing who gave it? How did you feel about receiving it?

2. Think of a gift of time, of caring, of help, of support that you have received recently—even if it was something you might not have paid particular attention to at

the time. Is there someone you would like to thank for that gift?

3. How does our culture encourage us to focus on what we do not have instead of celebrating the gifts that are already ours? What are some ways that you, as a Christian, can live against that cultural tide?

4. In Philippians 4:10-13, Paul offered his thanks for the support the Philippians had given him. How does this passage connect with the theme of this chapter? How do Paul's words capture your experience of gratitude?

5. What people in your life are you grateful for? How might you want to express your gratitude to them?

6. What are you grateful to God for? Consider writing a prayer of thanksgiving and reading it aloud to God.

chapter four

A Long Walk Home

They asked each other, "Were not our hearts
burning within us while he talked with us on the
road. . . ?" (Luke 24:32)

Life seems to drag when hope fades away. If Cleopas didn't know it before, it was clear to him that day. Plodding the road between Jerusalem and Emmaus, Cleopas and his friend may as well have been walking the path from joy to despair. It would be a long walk home.

These two followers of Jesus had been to Jerusalem for Passover. As usual, the celebration had involved a crush of people preparing to herd bleating lambs to the slaughter. The priests would have been up to their elbows in innocent blood as the people again remembered the deliverance God had provided their ancestors.

Cleopas had heard that Jesus was in the city. Perhaps he and his friend had even been part of the crowd that had welcomed Jesus with palms and hosannas on the previous Sunday. They no doubt had heard or seen Jesus before, since Luke gives us the clear impression that in some form they had been followers of Jesus. Cleopas may have hoped he might get a chance to see Jesus again, perhaps listen to another of his sermons. But when he at last saw Jesus, it was not the way he had planned.

There had been a trial. A crucifixion. Like a grisly counterweight to the glory and elation of the previous Sunday, the events of Friday had torn every shred of hope from Cleopas's heart. Every dream, every bit of confidence had been spiked to that wood, suspended amid the gathering darkness. Cleopas and his friend probably felt as if they had died there, too, along with Jesus. They had become silent witnesses to the death of joy.

There are times when sadness, loss, and hurt, crushed dreams, and buried ambition can transform life's journey from one of joy and wonder into something that feels more akin to the forced march of the condemned. Perhaps the cruelest passage of all is the moment when hope slips away. For Cleopas, there was nothing left but to acknowledge his disillusionment and go back to Emmaus.

The One in whom he had placed his hope was gone. The One he trusted had failed. Cleopas's longings for the future were as entombed as Jesus' lifeless body. As Cleopas made his way home, his only companions were the friend who walked in silence beside him and the disappointment he carried in his heart.

Cleopas isn't the only one who has walked that crowded path. So has Joyce. Joyce was a member of a congregation that I served early in my ministry. Over the years, long after we moved to different parts of the country, Joyce and I maintained contact. When I attended a conference in the Colorado mountains, near where Joyce lives, she offered to drive up and meet me during one of our afternoon breaks.

I asked Joyce what a tourist like me really should not miss, and she suggested a drive to the top of Hoover Pass from which we would be able to see valleys of quaking golden Aspens falling away at our feet and Quandary Peak towering above it all. I grabbed my binoculars, and we set off on our adventure to the top of the pass.

Two-thirds of the way up, the rain began to fall—in sheets. Reaching the crest, we pulled into the scenic area turn-off, the only car in the parking lot. Apparently, other tourists had observed the threatening clouds, the fog-shrouded peak, and had made a wiser choice. I figured it made sense to turn around and head back down; the weather didn't look as if it would be changing anytime soon. But we had come this far, and so, with the windshield wipers slapping away the rain, Joyce and I talked.

She had been struggling for quite some time with issues and events from years past, which continued to haunt her, sapping the joy from her life and affecting her marriage. She had been abused by a person she had trusted, betrayed by someone she had relied on to tell her the truth, someone who had fed her warped and twisted images of God to support his actions. Hidden deep within, Joyce still carried those lies that, like a sliver beneath the skin, had festered and infected her soul, leaving her with a frail and brittle faith. Here, beneath Quandary Peak, concealed behind the frowning clouds of an autumn storm, Joyce was in a quandary of her own. She wondered if she should just give up. She was angry with her life, with the circumstances of her existence, with a God who seemed to fail her and then desert her. Maybe, she wondered, the ability to trust God was a fool's hope, a pointless journey.

If you know what it's like to be discouraged, to have the wind sucked out of your hopes, then you've joined Joyce and Cleopas on the Emmaus road. I've walked it, too, and I've seen you there. I've noticed your footsteps ahead of me. It is a road littered with the burned-out wrecks of our desires, the abandoned hulks of our deepest hopes, the debris of ordinary living in all its underwhelming reality. It is a road we have all walked. Maybe you are walking it now.

Ordinary life contains its share of disappointment and discouragement. Sometimes they surface in a traumatic moment, a sudden gale of bad news. A marriage partner who promised to stay with you for life decides that forever is too long and leaves. Your long-held dream lies broken and scattered around you. You find yourself saying a final good-bye long before you ever dreamed you would. Traveling down a highway of hurt, you find yourself on the Emmaus road.

It is not always sudden tragedy, however, that places people on that path. Something as mundane as a string of too many days in which everything goes wrong can be enough to land us there. The daily stress of routine living builds until it hammers our heart and flattens our joy. Each week something serves as a reminder that we are locked into our situation and feel powerless to change it. And there we are on the Emmaus Road, walking the path of disappointment.

We would like to live above it all, escape the ordinary and find that place where disappointment can't touch us. But daily living rarely affords us that opportunity. It serves up discouragement as often as it does gladness. What can we do when we find ourselves carrying shattered hopes on a long, lonely walk?

Somewhere along the road, a third person overtook Cleopas and his friend. He explained to them what had happened. This person reminded them of God's centuries of promises. He assured them that Jesus was not dead; in fact, death itself had died. Focused on their own pain, at first they didn't recognize him. They walked and talked with him for miles without knowing in whose presence they were.

As they ate dinner together, they realized what the burning in their hearts meant: It was Jesus! The One who had carried their hopes into the grave had borne them back to life in a resurrection. In the midst of splintered hopes and unfulfilled dreams stood the One who could restore and renew all they had lost. In the course of a long walk home had come One who walked with them, who had the power to wipe away their troubled tears and make their lives new.

Seven miles. That's how far it is between Jerusalem and Emmaus. Cleopas and his friend managed to walk every one of them without recognizing Jesus. But their inability to identify him did not stop Jesus from showing up. In the same way he comes to us without waiting for us to recognize him. The thing that makes it possible for us to spot him is the fact that he is already there.

Cleopas's long walk home did not end with a broken heart. There is more to Joyce's story as well. The wipers began to squeak across dry glass as the rain stopped and the storm lifted, revealing first one mountain peak and then another. The valley below shimmered into view, and moments later Quandary Peak showed itself, wearing a dusting of fresh white snow on its crown. When Joyce and I finished marveling at the beauty, we began our drive down. But God wasn't done yet.

In front of us, arcing across the sky and touching down one switchback below us was a stunning rainbow unlike any I have ever seen. It was fat with colors that glowed with neon intensity against the dark spruce. The rainbow led us down the mountainside, not taking its leave until we had nearly reached town. On the way down I turned to Joyce with a simple question: "So, are you getting the message?"

Able to see only the rain, we had very nearly given up and missed the sun. With our trip appearing to be wasted energy, we might not have waited until the storm around Quandary Peak became a glistening rainbow. Some might call that remarkable moment a chance occurrence, a random combination of physical phenomena, but for those who see the world through the eyes of faith, that was Jesus appearing on the Emmaus road.

Life and faith are not so different from that afternoon on the mountain. When life tests the endurance of our faith, when the harsh realities of ordinary living cloud our days, we tend to see only the difficulties, and we risk missing the Son. When we find ourselves, our relationships, even our faith taking up residence in the shadow of our own personal Quandary Peak, we are tempted to quit too soon. When the rainbow comes, we're no longer there to see it.

A hurtful childhood, painful memories, a mountain storm, a long walk to Emmaus—Jesus does not always come to us easily recognized and free of all ambiguity. He meets us in unexpected ways, in unlikely circumstances: a fight with our spouse, a strained relationship, a threat to our health, searing memories. And it is there, contrary to all our expectations, that we are most deeply connected with Christ, with the One who understands suffering. The painful parts of life are where we will find Jesus.

Even when we cannot recognize Jesus along the road, we can still trust him. Even when we cannot understand what is happening, we can still hold onto him. The love he offers is not a phantom; that voice is not the wind. All the promise, all the love, all the hope . . . it is right there with us on the Emmaus road.

When everyday life churns out disappointment, when what is normal and routine and business-as-usual produces discouragement, when you find yourself on your way to Emmaus, remember the words of two lonely men on a lonely road when they were met by a stranger: "Did we not feel our hearts burning within us?"

Some Things to Think About

1. Think of a time when your hopes got shattered. What were the circumstances? How did you feel?

2. Who came alongside you to help you through that time? How did you recognize that their help was what you needed?

3. What kinds of circumstances are most likely to cause you to experience the kind of spiritual turmoil that

---

Cleopas felt? What keeps you from recognizing Jesus' presence at a time like that? What would help you recognize him?

4. Describe a time in your life when you felt like giving up. Can you think of any "rainbows" that appeared, signaling that God's presence was still with you?

5. If you are suffering over something right now, what do you want to say to Jesus?

6. Have you ever had an experience of feeling your heart "burning within"? What were the circumstances and with whom did you share it?

The God Who Knows
What to Do

"Our friend Lazarus has fallen asleep; but I am
going there to wake him up." (John 11:11)

Agnes made it clear: I was to offer a prayer at her sister's
graveside and nothing else. Her sister had died in Florida,
and Agnes was calling to ask (more to the point, *inform*)
me concerning the prayer I would say at the cemetery.
Agnes said she would be present with a handful of out-
of-town guests.

"How about a Psalm?" I offered. "Or a Scripture
reading?"

Agnes interrupted. "No. I said I want only a prayer."

In her nineties and stern as iron, Agnes had always
intimidated me. I didn't argue; a prayer it would be.

Saturday arrived and I went to the cemetery, but I
could find no Agnes. The cemetery was webbed with
curving roads and paths. After driving past the same
small group of people three times, I stopped and asked
if they happened to be Agnes' relatives. Yes, they were,
they said, and though I did not know it, Agnes had gone
into the hospital and would not be with us.

Using my keen pastoral intuition, I quickly discerned that this little group was expecting something more than a simple prayer. What was I supposed to do? As I prepared to launch into an impromptu memorial service, one of the group suddenly, silently pushed a cardboard box toward me. Written on a label across the top of the box was a name: Cecelia. Taking a quick glance inside, I realized it *was* Cecelia, or at least her ashes contained in a plastic bag.

Things were becoming more confusing by the moment. Agnes had left no instructions as to what was supposed to happen after the prayer. There was no urn, no grave, and no Agnes, but there were some family members who were definitely waiting for something to happen. I fumbled through portions of the standard graveside service, but I was uncertain what to do next. Assuming Agnes had something in mind, I put Cecelia under my arm and headed for the car. My next stop would be the hospital.

I donned my most compassionate pastoral expression as I entered Agnes's room, only to see her sit bolt upright in bed, pointing a bony finger at me as I came through the door.

"What are you doing here?"

"Well, I heard you were hospitalized, and I thought I'd stop by and see you."

"Where are the ashes?" she demanded.

"Um, in my car." I was worried Agnes was about to come across the room and cane me.

"My relatives called me from the cemetery and told me you took Cecelia with you. What are you doing driving around with her in your car? You get back to the cemetery right now and take Cecelia with you. The grave diggers are waiting to bury her, and they'll charge me extra if they have to wait much longer."

Turning on my heels, I dashed back to the cemetery where Cecelia was properly buried, the guests were still confused, and I was just relieved to go home.

Throughout the confusing day, with each new twist in Cecelia's strange adventure, one question kept popping up in my mind: What was I supposed to do? Given the way humanity deals with death, perhaps it wasn't such an unusual question.

Death is the one thing in life we don't know what to do with.

The other day I went to the grocery store, but instead of picking up bread and milk, I collected some headlines from the magazine racks. It is hard to avoid the trashy teasers and the models with their sultry gazes while waiting to pay for groceries. "Tips for Healthy Living" proclaimed one issue. In big, bold letters another offered "Top Ten Fixes for Skin over Thirty-Five." One magazine promised "Get Sexy Thighs Fast." Hmm, I wondered, what's wrong with my thighs? The next one claimed that it contained the "Definitive Guide to Amazing Abs." I thought, my abs are pretty amazing; they're just not visible beneath the layers of insulation I carry. And then there were the headlines, each in a different magazine, that all seemed to be written by the same person: "Natural Ways to Boost Your Health," "Boost Your Energy Level," "Lose Weight, Boost Your Satisfaction." I suppose with baby-boomers well into middle age, just about everything needs a boost.

Publishers may think they are selling diets and sex appeal. They may even think they're selling magazines. What they are really selling is a perspective on life, a promise that, with the right plan, discipline, and attention, we can preserve life and retain our youth. It's an image we are more than happy to accept. We are reassured by the idea of a life we can securely hold on to. We are eager for the promise of life that never creaks or hobbles toward an inevitable decline. We want to be protected from the threats of an intruder whose name we do not even wish to speak.

Still, behind the headlines about grabbing and holding onto the gusto in life, anxiety lurks. Beyond the swagger, there's a shudder. Beneath the confidence, there's a cold sweat. Between the words of defiance that trumpet an eternal youth echoes the hollow sound of dread. We would do anything to pretend that death is not waiting for us. We don't know what to do with it.

Death is the stalker of dreams. Prowling through the corridors of life, it hides in the shadows of our existence. It creeps just beyond the fringe of consciousness, waiting. Waiting for its opportunity to render our accomplishments meaningless. Biding its time until that moment when it will empty the joy from our hearts and steal the song from our lips, leaving in their places silent tongues and tear-flooded cheeks.

Death is a testimony to the futility of our struggles. Our quest for significance in life, our desire to leave a legacy, to fulfill dreams, to rise above the ordinary is, at its heart, a battle with death.

If you have ever strolled along the breakers in Newport, Rhode Island, you've seen the mansions. Their gold leaf shimmers in the sunlight, and the floor-to-ceiling windows look out on manicured lawns. Inside, their massive staircases soar upward, greeting you as you step through the door. The now-silent ballrooms once hosted the social gatherings of prominent people. The opulence of every detail whispers, "Here was grandeur. Here was wealth. Here was success."

Today, most of the mansions in Newport are tourist attractions. The rooms once filled with debutantes, industrial giants, and wealthy matrons now host tourists sporting T-shirts and plaid shorts. The glory of those who built these homes for themselves has been replaced by college students working as summer guides in buildings maintained as historic sites. The monumental wealth it took to build these castles is dispersed among scattered descendants. Now, a fifteen-dollar ticket gains you entrance to watch actors recreating a bygone era.

Death turns our brief lives into nothing more than a hiccup in time, a nanosecond in which we try to build something that will endure. The plans made, the projects undertaken, the need to acquire experiences—all are a part of the mad dash for meaning. Anything that will anchor us more firmly to life or fill us with a sense of significance feeds the illusion that death can be supplanted by a list of accomplishments.

We focus much of our life on a futile effort to take out a restraining order against death. Uncertain how to deal with it, we pretend death is something that happens to someone else, not to us. Or we say that death is just another season of life. But it is not one of the seasons of life; it is the end of seasons. Nothing we do stops us from dying. Nothing we accomplish prevents us from presiding over personal little funerals at which we bury our dreams or say good-bye to our hopes. Even the act of living from day to day contains its share of daily dying.

When our children were younger, the night before Easter always brought a certain amount of sadness to our home. Easter is an unusually busy weekend for a pastor and his family, so we rarely managed to color Easter eggs until late Saturday night. After days of waiting, our children would gather around the kitchen table, bowls of blue and red dye at the ready. But as eggs are prone to do, some would break as we decorated them, and, of course, an egg once broken is not much use for coloring or keeping. The saddest part of the evening was that, nearly without exception, every egg that failed to survive belonged to Jeff. Tears would well up in his little eyes and a small voice would plead, "Why do things like this always happen to me?" I could feel my heart twist, for there was nothing at that late hour a mother or father could do to make things better. A child waits all year to color eggs, and then one after another they break and fall useless into the trash.

Our lives, and all we work so hard to achieve, are a little like those scattered shells. What are we supposed to do when shattered dreams lie at our feet? When the look on the doctor's face tells us more than we want to know? When the telephone rings at night, and our children are in danger or our parents are sick? When our spouse says, "I don't love you anymore," or our boss says, "I don't need you anymore," or our emotions tell us, "It's not worth trying anymore"? I don't know what to do with a life fissured with little marks of death any more than I knew what to do with Jeff's broken eggs or poor Cecelia's ashes.

But Jesus does. Jesus knows what to do. He knew what to do for Lazarus. When we read this story, most of us focus on Jesus, Mary, and Martha. Preachers build entire sermons on that shortest of biblical verses, "Jesus wept." Commentaries attempt to plumb the depths of why Jesus waited so long to come to the aid of his friends, and they analyze the sisters' statements of faith. Much is made of the strategic location of this incident as the gateway to the Passion story, and how this last, greatest miracle turned the quiet opposition to Jesus into a conspiracy planning his death.

In all of this, we tend to overlook one person, perhaps because what he did was so natural, so ordinary. Maybe we miss him because he reminds us so much of ourselves. We forget about Lazarus! His great claim to fame was that he died. Lazarus doesn't come to mind for any impressive deed of faith or admirable sacrifice made for his Lord. The truth is, there is only a single reason we know Lazarus's name at all. One day his lungs stopped breathing and his heart went silent. That's when Jesus stepped in and raised him. In John's entire Gospel, that's all Lazarus ever did to distinguish himself, that's the only legacy he left behind: He died, and Jesus raised him.

Think about it: What would you like to achieve in your life? What would you like to be remembered for? The accomplishments we struggle to amass, the recognition we fight to obtain, the things we do to try and rise above the ordinary and find the joy we think we're missing—they all pale in comparison to the promise of the resurrection. Despite what the magazines would have us believe, in the face of a culture that marginalizes any discussion of heaven, the paradox the gospel reveals is that the very reason we can delight in living today is because we know we will die . . . and we know what awaits us, and who. The knowledge that our time is limited and our future secure, rather than being a cause for frantic existence, means we are free to live in joy.

When Jesus stands at the tomb and calls, "Come out!" it is our name on his lips. That voice among the gravestones means an end to despair, bathing life in unsurpassable purpose, infusing it with joy. No longer must the experience of daily living bear the crushing weight of all our hopes and dreams. The musts and oughts and fears in life can become less urgent, less terrifying, in the security of realizing that when the chips are down and death has crushed all for which we have worked, Jesus knows what to do. That is ultimate good news for a dead man called Lazarus, a woman whose name was Cecelia, and a confused pastor named Joe—and for you.

Recently, our congregation gathered for worship. It was the second Sunday after Christmas, and we were in the midst of sharing communion together. The promise repeated softly through the air: "This is the body of Christ, given for you. This is the blood of Christ, shed for you."

Having finished communing a row of people, I paused, waiting for the rest of the team to catch up.

"Given for you . . . shed for you . . ."

Out of the corner of my eye, I noticed a single leaf from the poinsettias left over from Christmas drift silently to the floor. It was dead. Its life was over. It had accomplished its decorating purpose, and after worship it would be swept up and tossed out. What had once been beautiful was now lifeless. Useless. Throw it away. That's what you do with dead leaves.

"This is the blood . . . shed for you."

The contrast struck me. A leaf had fallen to the floor in the middle of a festival of death and resurrection. What we were celebrating, the words that echoed through the air, contained the promise that when we die we won't simply be swept out of the way. Our death, as natural and expected as that of the poinsettia leaf, occurs within the reality of a God who breaks and gives himself to us so that our eternal life is assured.

Those words that we say and hear so often took on a powerful meaning for me in that moment. God's guarantee of eternal life in Christ sheds a new light on all that seems ordinary. Ours is a deeper definition of success. There is no dream to chase that will give us greater joy. We have the promise of resurrection. God knows what to do, and it is enough.

Some Things to Think About

1. Think of the most recent funeral you attended. How did the people around you speak about death? What thoughts did you have about death?

2. In what ways is the drive for accomplishment, success, or recognition a hedge against death?

3. If you could talk to someone with a terminal illness, how do you imagine they would say their life has changed in finding out their time is limited? In what way does the promise of the resurrection impact those changes?

4. Reflect on this sentence from the chapter as it relates to the promise of the resurrection: "No longer must the experience of daily living bear the crushing weight of all our hopes and dreams." Think of a specific way this week you could live as if this statement were true. How might that increase the joy in your life?

5. Think of a recent situation where you didn't know what to do next. To whom did you turn for help?

----

6. How much do you trust God to know what to do? Does it feel like "enough" for you? Consider writing a letter to God, expressing what you trust and what you don't trust. Ask God for reassurance about the promise of resurrection.

chapter six

The Joy
of Deep Waters

[Jesus] said, "Go, sell everything you have and give it to the poor, and you will have treasure in heaven. Then come, follow me." At this the man's face fell. He went away sad because he had great wealth. (Mark 10:21-22)

Every now and then I'm reminded of how much time I spend playing in the shallows of life—and faith.

When I was a kid, my family spent many summer weekends camping in Wisconsin with my relatives. One year, as my cousin and I were out exploring, we discovered a pool of water from which a small stream ran. We immediately decided to do what any kid would do in that situation: We became instant engineers and set to work damming up the stream at its source. We gathered up rocks and branches and piled them across the mouth of the little stream at the point where it escaped the pool, filling in the cracks with mud and debris. But when we stood back to view our handiwork, we noticed that the level of water in the pool had risen until it was flowing over the top of the dam.

There was nothing to do but tear it apart and repeat the process, adding more sticks and handfuls of mud, but

---

no matter what we did, the level of water always rose until it flowed over and around our barricade. We spent hours demolishing and rebuilding until we finally realized that the little pool was fed by a natural spring, a source of deep water. That was when the fun really began.

As we watched the water gurgle up from far below the surface, we finally found the courage to put our hands in the center of the spring and feel the water bubble around our fingers. We pushed our hands in deeper, up to our elbows, and then deeper still until we had sunk our arms in up to our shoulders, and still we could not touch the bottom of the spring. We reached as far down as we could, but the water came from a source deeper still.

The shallows of the stream had been interesting enough at first. They were, after all, what had first caught our attention. But the real fun was playing in the endlessly deep, constantly gushing spring.

It is so easy to live life on the surface, allowing ourselves to bob along in the shallows. We expend enormous amounts of energy trying to figure out how to make our lives more manageable, how to keep everything afloat as we try to balance all we want to do, or feel we need to do, or think we ought to be doing. We're endlessly looking for ways to make things more convenient, find more pleasure in our days, fill the emptiness that gnaws away at our insides, or make daily life a little more exciting and a little less tedious.

We would like to give ourselves over to a purpose bigger than our own wants and desires, if we could only find the time. We'd love to experience a profound closeness to God, if we could only squeeze it in. We know there is more to faith and life, but like little kids playing near a spring, we spend more time building dams and trying to direct the flow of life than we do plunging ourselves into the holy depths of discipleship. Jesus invites us to submerge ourselves in the source of all things, but instead, we try to control and contain

God's claim on our lives so it won't overwhelm our little boats. When we live in the shallows, ordinary living feels superficial because we spend so much of it on the surface.

He could be you. He could be me. He was a would-be follower of Jesus, a disciple wanna-be. His heart urged him forward, but his fear pushed him to play it safe. He was torn between sticking with Jesus and sticking with the life he knew. His choice was a simple, if difficult one: hold fast to the image of security or cash everything in on the strength of a promise; play on the surface or dive in deep.

Mark tells us about him in chapter ten. He was a wealthy man in search of something more. He'd made it in life; he had all he needed. He was the person we envy, the rare individual whom good fortune has decided to embrace. If you asked him how his family was, he'd say they're great. His business? Never better. How about his health? He probably looked lean and fit with a body that appeared ten years younger than his age. His life was together, yet he still felt incomplete.

Deep in his heart rustled an uneasy restlessness, a vague sense of something not quite right. His approach to Jesus gave him away. Perhaps this traveling teacher would have the clue to what he sought. When he found Jesus, he blurted out his worry: "Good teacher, what must I do to inherit eternal life?"

Jesus' answer was not exactly what the rich man had in mind. He had not been counting on this! Jesus told him to give it all up. Cash everything in on a promise of future gain. Trade it in for a ticket to paradise. Then, come follow.

In one awful, tragic moment, the man's face fell, his smile faded. He set his chin, turned his back, and walked away. The price was too high, the risk too great. The man found himself pulled taut between Jesus' challenge and his own timidity. He was torn between that which he most wanted and that which he most feared.

Perhaps you are acquainted with that kind of tension. You've contemplated making a career change, but the financial ramifications are daunting. You're considering moving to a new community, but it would require leaving friends and family behind. You're wondering if you should take a chance on that new relationship, but what if it didn't work out?

I remember when our oldest son, Jeff, was just beginning to venture to our neighborhood swimming pool. Together we would head for the pool, his face bright with the excitement of our imminent adventure. I would jump right in, but Jeff stood there on the side. He wanted to enter the water, yet he still had a child's fear of it.

I urged him and comforted him, offering gentle words of encouragement. I showed him it was safe and promised to hold him tight. I did everything I could think of. Still he stood on the edge, too uncertain to jump in. He wanted so desperately to make the splashing leap that tears came to his eyes. We endured this tension together trip after trip to the pool. I found in my heart a deep sadness and pain for my child who wanted something so badly, something I could give, but whose fear would not allow him to accept it.

That was years ago now. Today Jeff is a strong swimmer. He's taken lifeguard classes, and I would not hesitate to call for him if I needed a rescue. After all the torture of indecision, Jeff found the courage to risk his safety for the promise of something better. He traded in the edge of the pool, which would forever be secure but unsatisfying, for the joy of deep water.

That's what it came down to for the rich man, just as it does for us. We do an injustice to this story if we think that Jesus' challenge to the man had to do only with giving away his wealth. At a deeper level, the decision he faced involved something far more significant than a few coins in the bank. The heart of the matter was this: Was he willing to go deep?

Jesus' call is not only to let go of our nickels and dimes, but to release the death grip we hold on the control panel of our lives, that we might become dependent on him. In inviting us to follow, Jesus asks us to detach ourselves from the life we have struggled so mightily to build, so that we are free to attach ourselves to him. But we harbor a fear deep within us, a powerful reluctance to loosen our hold on our own self-sufficiency.

We drag into Jesus' presence all the things we've deemed important in life, but he says to us as he did to the rich man, "Let go. Give it up. Let go of trying to hold onto a life that is forever slipping through your fingers. Give up allowing the circumstances of the moment, or the balance in your checkbook, or your worry about tomorrow to hold hostage the joy I would give you. Be done with the notion that you can split the difference, putting one foot in the Kingdom while keeping the other firmly planted in the world."

In the conversation between the rich man and Jesus, Mark recounts an interesting detail. He tells us that Jesus "looked at him and loved him." Jesus' response is the same for us. Jesus doesn't condemn. He doesn't thunder damnation or level accusations or guilt us into a deeper involvement with him. He neither denounces, blames, nor rebukes us. He simply loves us.

Jesus invites us into the depths where we discover his endless love bubbling up all around us. The deeper we go, the more profoundly we come into contact with him, the more we come to recognize him standing at the heart of all we are and all we dream, all we say and all we do, all we desire and all we live for. Jesus means to captivate us with his love, not crush us with new demands. It is his love that sets us free to risk following him, for risk-taking comes only from being loved.

My wife, Barbie, and I first met when we worked together in a residential treatment center for adolescent girls. Barbie worked the day shift; I was the night staff. Each morning my shift overlapped hers for a half hour. During those times, we began to talk. It wasn't long before I wanted in the worst way to ask her out. But I'm the timid type, and I was afraid. Perhaps she would say no, or worse yet, maybe she would laugh at such an absurd idea. I told myself she might be seeing someone else. I was so reluctant to risk my self-esteem that I didn't even realize she was offering me inviting hints. She told me how she loved the state fair and happened to have a couple of tickets. I didn't pick up on the clue. She must mean she's going with someone else, I thought. Finally, fed up with waiting for me to act, she invited me out, and I readily accepted.

My uncertainty about Barbie's feelings toward me prevented me from risking any part of myself. Once convinced of her love, however, things moved along rather nicely; I asked her to marry me one month later, and our wedding took place four months after that.

The courage to risk comes not by command but as the result of love. Only when we know we are loved, when we believe it, when we are as certain of it as we are of life itself, will we hazard our hearts.

How certain are you, in the deepest recesses of your well-protected heart, that God loves you, that God has a deep, abiding affection for you? Sure, you learned that in Sunday school. But do you ever fear whether you are good enough to hold onto God's love? Do you *really* understand that God loves not just the easily acceptable parts of you—the parts you are proud of—but also the parts that leave you ashamed and horrified? Can you grasp the reality of a love that is so great that God's heart breaks when you are in pain? Can you let yourself believe that simply the *thought* of you brings a sparkle of delight to God's eyes?

It is this certain knowledge of God's incredible, unwavering, ferocious passion for you that will ignite the courage within you to risk following Jesus. The subtle joy of an ordinary day is that it presents yet another opportunity to risk giving and receiving love, to experience the thrill of trusting yourself to the One who adores you. You can keep your heart closed down and protected, or you can open it up. You can hold on to what you hope will keep you safe, or you can take steps, however timid they may seem, to follow Jesus down the path he would lead you.

It's a risk, to be sure. It's always a risk to forgo the shallows and splash in the deep. But if you're not sure it's worth it, if you don't think it will uncover a deep wellspring of joy, let me suggest you check with a young man I know who is heading out the door right now to enjoy a swim.

Some Things to Think About

1. What were some of the risks you took as a kid? What were some things you decided *not* to risk?

2. Describe a time as an adult when you chose taking a risk over staying "safe." What or who helped you take the risk?

3. What are some of the things in your life that seem to provide security, that you want to hang on to?

4. What do you feel you need to let go of in order to follow Jesus further?

5. Name some of the things that cause you to begin to doubt God's love. Consider beginning a list of the promises of Jesus, of Scripture, that affirm God's endless love for you.

6. How would you describe the connection between risk and joy?

chapter seven

Grace Matters

Jesus straightened up and asked her, "Woman, where are they? Has no one condemned you?"

"No one, sir," she said.

"Then neither do I condemn you," Jesus declared. "Go now and leave your life of sin." (John 8:10-11)

I discovered grace in my garage the other day. A young man was eyeing my bicycle as if he had just stumbled across a winning lottery ticket. He lifted it up to check its weight and pronounced it the lightest bike he had ever seen. He stepped back to admire the cherry-red tubes and the graceful curve of the handlebars, then lifted it again as if he couldn't believe his luck.

"How much do you want for it?" he asked, as he spun the wheels and tested the brakes.

"Twenty-five bucks," I said. This was, after all, a garage sale.

"Would you take twenty? It's all I've got."

"Sure," I shrugged. I just wanted to get rid of it; it was taking up too much space. I probably would have let him have it for free. The bicycle had been hanging in my garage, dusty and forgotten, for years. It had been ages since I last rode it because I had acquired much nicer, sleeker machines. It was old. The shifters were dated, not all the gears worked correctly, the rubber was worn and brittle from having been ridden too many miles, too long ago. Far from being the svelte frame he hefted into the air, the bike had all the weight savings of a Hummer. In its day it had been a nice, not an outstanding, bike. But now it was not worth very much . . . except to the young man in front of me. To him, it was worth all he had.

When he looked at it, he did not see an old bike whose best days were behind it, with a ratty seat and mismatched components. He saw the object of his dreams. He saw a lightweight racing machine—and his own good fortune for having the opportunity to spend more money on it than he should, for to him it was worth all that and more. He saw the most beautiful bicycle ever made, and no disclaimers on my part would convince him otherwise. He hopped on and pedaled down the street toward home, astride a bike that had suddenly been transformed from my useless junk into a machine with new purpose and new significance.

I think that's something close to what grace is: a young man buying an old bicycle and delighting in the beauty he sees in it. Grace is knowing that you are a worn-out bike, out of date, far too heavy, your value suspect; but then Jesus wanders into the yard and, barely containing his excitement, offers to buy you for more than you're worth so he can take you home, clean you up, and restore your reason and purpose.

We are created for grace. It's not that we are given grace as a last resort, in a panicky, last-ditch, everything-else-has-been-tried bid to keep us off the scrap heap. No, we are created for grace. That is the relationship for which we are born. The Savior loves us, not in spite of our creaking integrity or marred surface, and certainly not because of our continual attempts to appear to be more than we are. Jesus delights in us because we are the object of his desire. He sees in us all the potential that has been neglected and forgotten and worn out along the way. He recognizes in us all the goodness and life that is in him and takes us home, chipped paint, squeaky chain and all. Grace is what guarantees that in all our charmless charm and empty, desperate need, we count. Our life matters.

Significance is one of joy's key ingredients. Look around at the public buildings named after presidents, at the statue of the hero in the local park, at the legacies people seek to leave behind. We want our lives to count for something; we want our days to signify something more valuable than the sum of their parts. We want our existence to stand for something more enduring than personal happiness, more compelling than individual success, more important than stacking up well against those to whom we compare ourselves. A joyful life is one that is marked with significance, that is confident of its worth.

We live, however, in a Catch-22. On the one hand, everywhere we turn, we are greeted with a long list of ingredients for the good life, leaving us exhausted from the effort at reaching for something that is forever, maddeningly beyond our grasp. We spend much of our time acutely aware of the discrepancy between our perceptions of success and the level of our performance. We are chained to an endless effort to act good, look good, feel good, *be* good, in the hopes of establishing the value of our life.

But on the other hand, we're not long content with what we own or drive or wear, or even what we achieve, because, as desperately as we want those things to make us happy, they are ultimately powerless to bring meaning to our lives. If we live with a low-grade dissatisfaction with routine life, if deep-seated joy evades our grasp, perhaps it is because our world whispers a malignant message that what we have is not enough, that who we are is insufficient.

That is where grace comes in.

Certainly, the woman John tells us about in chapter eight, who stumbled into Jesus' presence a few seconds ahead of a murderous crowd, mattered—at least to Jesus.

John provides us with scant background on the woman. We are told it was early morning—dawn, in some translations—when the officials brought her before Jesus. Apparently, she had spent the night with someone other than her husband and had been caught in the act. John tells us nothing else, only that she had broken the law in committing adultery, for which the punishment was stoning. Her life was no longer of value, so said the religious leaders; what worth she may have had, she had sacrificed to a misguided moment of pleasure, a flagrant breaking of the law.

We might imagine that the woman was the victim of an abusive husband, seeking solace in the arms of an understanding friend, that the romantic liaison was an unfortunate and unplanned accident. We could suppose she was a bored spouse, looking for a thrill and ready to dally with anyone sporting a beard and willing to take up with her. But Jesus did not question the factors that gave rise to the incident, nor seek justifications that would explain it. He seemed concerned only that standing before him was a woman in need not of condemnation but compassion, not of reproach but release. He saw not what she had done but who she was. Suddenly, instead of the officials' judgment hanging over her guilty head like a sword, Jesus' mercy washed over her like a hot shower on a cold morning. With a single sentence Jesus forgave her, affirmed her worth, declared her significance to him, and invited her into a whole new life. And in that moment grace arrived, unexpected, for a person in desperate need of it.

Living in grace matters because it is grace that marks our lives as meaningful. And that, in turn, is a key to joy. Our societal fixation with self-esteem aside, it is grace that reminds us that God loved us before we could do anything to engender that love, before we could plan out our life, before we could succeed at anything. God loves us when our future spreads in front of us like an endless vista of possibilities, and God loves us still when every option has vanished and life has been squeezed down to its barest essentials.

The late Rich Mullins, a singer/songwriter whose lyrics are powerful testaments to the grace and goodness of Christ, was fond of saying that what we believe makes us who we are. If we believe that our identity and our purpose is based on what we do, how we look, and how much money we have, that inevitably shapes who we become . . . and we become people of shallow dreams, shrunken possibilities, and withered joy.

In reality, however, none of that forms the foundation of our truest identity. We were created for eternity, we have been shaped by grace, we were bought at a price, and God's desire for us is that we will live with him beyond the day when the galaxies burn out. Our truest identity is that we are children of God and inheritors of eternal life.

Grace sets us free from having to appear to be good enough to make the grade, freeing us to live fully and in forgiveness. It releases us from the crooked, accusing finger of self-condemnation, allowing us to gobble up God's mercy as one who hasn't eaten for days. As it did for the woman who stood before Jesus with nothing to offer but her panicked heart, grace invites us to step out from under the heaviness of all the blaming, all the guilt, all the shame, all the gnawing sense that we're just not good enough, into the buoyancy of Christ's creative love.

Jesus' words—"Neither do I condemn you. Go now and leave your life of sin"—contain an acceptance for which we do not have to be worthy, forgiveness we do not have to deserve, hope we do not have to buy, and love we can never lose. Never again must we go alone through this life trying to measure up or condemning ourselves when we do not.

Our value is secure. Our significance is certain. What could we ever do, buy, or accomplish that could enhance that intrinsic worth? From what source could there spring a more profound joy?

Some Things to Think About

1. What are the "standards" to which you hold yourself now? Think of your family, your work, your church, your neighborhood.

2. What makes it difficult for you to treat yourself with grace?

3. In what ways does the manner in which Jesus dealt with the adulterous woman help you face your own brokenness?

4. How does Jesus' delight over you, just as you are, give you the freedom to grow and change?

5. Take some time to ponder this idea of Jesus seeing you as beautiful and of value. What emotions surface as you consider this? How might this truth affect how you see other people?

6. Think of someone who is worn-out or not very appealing. What could you do for them that would reflect Jesus' way of seeing them?

chapter eight

Hidden Jesus

[Zacchaeus] . . . wanted to see who Jesus was, but being a short man he could not, because of the crowd. So he ran ahead and climbed a sycamore-fig tree to see him, since Jesus was coming that way. (Luke 19:3-4)

Perhaps you remember Zacchaeus. He's every Sunday school child's hero. I grew up singing odes to his diminutive stature and gazing at flannel-graphs depicting his climb up a sycamore tree so he could catch a glimpse of Jesus. That's what intrigues me about his story. He wanted to see Jesus. So do I.

Sometimes I think that if I could just get a glimpse of Jesus, my faith would become anything but routine. If I could just catch a flash of his robe as he passed, if our eyes could meet even for an instant, it would be enough to banish the ordinary sameness of my pretty average faith. How could discipleship ever seem flat or bland after you've seen Jesus? I'd climb a tree for that, wouldn't you?

But Jesus isn't always so easy to see. It's not so simple for a modern-day Zacchaeus to scramble up a tree and watch for Jesus to look up and call us by name. Might be sitting there a long time. Might be waiting a whole life-time for him to go by. When our lives are smothered in layers of daily routine, when our spiritual senses are suffo-cated under brutal commutes and relentless job demands, when a coarse culture or endless personal choices blunt our God awareness, is it even possible for us to encoun-ter Jesus in our everyday lives? Can we hope to spot him tracking across the landscape of our regular days?

I haven't seen him yet. Or have I?

Each year the high school youth from our congrega-tion go to Mexico to build houses for those whose cur-rent housing consists of scrap lumber, cardboard boxes, and a little plaster. Most years, I accompany the group. We camp for the week in what was once a gravel pit, and each morning at 6 A.M. we head out for a day of work. It's dirty business.

In fact, dirt is the one thing we can count on during our mission week. Overcast skies may soften the blunt force of the sun, or the air may carry a freshening breeze, but the dirt remains. A shower at the end of the day, con-sisting of cold water from a bucket, rinses it away only momentarily. Dirt covers everything with its fine grit. It works its way into every crack, every fold. It covers every surface. There is no escaping it. It is as pervasive as e-mail spam, and about as welcome.

Much of our work in Mexico seems to involve dirt. The ground has to be dug up, or filled in, to level the site for the foundation. The first and last day of the work week involves the continuous hand mixing of cement and rock and sand—just other forms of dirt, if you ask me—to produce the concrete and the stucco. Maybe that's why finding Jesus hidden in the dirt seemed so significant.

This "hidden Jesus" turned up at one of the work sites on the first day of construction that year. About mid-morning, as the group was digging at one end of the site in order to prepare it for pouring the concrete slab, one of the students discovered a picture in a shovel of dirt. Having been buried under ground, it was torn and tattered, but it revealed the face of Jesus. Someone from the group spotted it, brushed it off, flattened it out, and attached it to a nearby fence as inspiration. Hidden Jesus—you couldn't see him at first, covered as he was by the dirt, but he was there all along.

We returned home after a week that was as astonishing in its joy as it was dirty in its living conditions; as stunning in its depth of community as it was grueling in its labor; as covered by the Spirit-breath of God as it was covered by the dirt of Mexico. And then came the hard part. Among a flurry of e-mails, some of our adult participants put it this way:

> "I'm having trouble letting go of our week . . . can't really concentrate on my work today because it seems rather meaningless. Sadly enough, I'm sure by week's end I'll be back to 'normal,' fretting with everyone else over things that won't matter in a month."

> "I sit here at work trying to get back into the stream of things . . . you know, calls to clients, files to reopen, reports to finish. . . ."

It's easy to see Jesus when you can climb a sycamore and rise above the crowd, where there are no distractions, no competing demands, nothing to disturb your vantage point. But most of life isn't like that. Most of life is a jumble of obligations and desires that threaten to knock us out of our tree or lead us ever further away from the One we most want to see. There is no escaping life's dirt.

There have been times in my life when my faith has seemed dry and brittle, my prayers listless, my worship dull. There have been times when the cares of the day have blown my faith away like dust in the wind, and I have felt alone, or like Zacchaeus, a very small person lost in a very large crowd. It's at those moments that my vision of Jesus has blurred. My head has been filled with other desires, and my eyes have been focused elsewhere. Those are the times when Jesus has become a "something" to me rather than Someone, an object of doctrines and practices rather than a Savior willing to offer himself in relationship to me.

The secret to excavating life's joy lies in learning to identify the hidden Jesus amid the dirt.

Denise wasn't expecting to hear from Jesus the day her phone rang, no more than Lynne was anticipating Jesus on the other end of the line when she dialed. But that's often the way it is with Jesus. He shows up on a weekday afternoon in the midst of our most common routines. He comes in unpredictable packages, in unforeseen forms. He catches us by surprise because he looks so ordinary. He turns up in everyday people, tripping us up with his unexpected goodness, and then he changes our lives.

The day Lynne called, Denise had been struggling. Denise is a mom with two small children, and as any parent can tell you, young kids have a way of breaking you down after a while. They are compact packages of energy demanding constant attention, with an uncanny ability to force you to live their lives rather than your own. They can turn your heart into a churning cauldron of love and frustration, joy and aggravation, delight and desperation.

On the day the phone rang, Denise was slogging through some pretty trying times. Her dad had been ill, and it seemed that life had become little more than a series of problems to be coped with. You probably know what that feels like: The clouds boil up and turn your spirits gray, and you feel as if you're a little speck in a big world filled with other people's agendas. But when Denise picked up the phone, it was Lynne on the other end of the line.

Denise didn't know who Lynne was. Lynne explained that she was a member of Christ Lutheran Church and, as a part of the Capital Campaign, some members of the congregation were taking on the challenge of praying for each and every person on the roster. Lynne explained that she had Denise's name and was calling to see if there were anything specific for which she could pray.

"You can't imagine the day I've had," Denise responded. "Do you know what it's like to have a seven-year-old and a two-year-old?"

Lynn said she certainly could; her own children were the same ages. She offered to pray about that.

Denise mentioned that she missed the support of the mom's group she had given up because of her father's illness, and Lynn spoke of the group available for her at the church. Not ten minutes before, Denise admitted, she had prayed for God to help her, to give her something to get her through these tough times . . . and then Lynne called. "You don't even know me," Denise said, "and yet you took the time to call. I just asked God to help, and he gave me you."

Later, as Denise shared her story with me, she described Lynne as a well-timed gift, a blessing from God, an answer to prayer, a hidden Jesus. "Sometimes," she said, "when you think you're pretty unimportant, too insignificant for God to notice, God reminds you that you are important, and lets you know that you are loved and cared for."

"I felt so loved," Denise continued, "I hadn't been going to church lately, but Lynne called me and prayed for me anyway. It reminded me that even though I've been gone for a while, you have all still been there, being faithful. I have felt blessed ever since. It has changed me."

Now, if you asked Lynne, she would be a little embarrassed about all that.

Calling people to pray for them was pushing her way outside her comfort zone, and when she picked up the phone, expecting—even hoping—to simply leave a message on a machine, it turned out that the first person she called was Denise.

If for Denise, Lynne was the presence of Jesus, then for Lynne, Denise was the same, because Lynne had other calls to make, and Denise's response gave her the encouragement she needed to follow through with the rest. And for me? Well, sometimes preachers go dry. At least this one does. I go to the well looking to draw up buckets of inspiration, and I find myself still parched and dusty, certain that I have nothing to say and no way to say it, feeling like Zacchaeus and wondering why Jesus is so hard to see. It was that kind of day when Lynne and Denise shared their story with me, and then I saw him. It wasn't only Lynne and Denise at whom I was looking; it was Jesus bringing fresh life and blessing to me.

Sometimes, on a good day, it is easy to find Jesus. Someone hugs us or holds our hand, communicating our value and reminding us that we are loved, and there stands Jesus, wrapping his arms around us. A friend offers words of encouragement and support, and they are Jesus' own words speaking deeply into the most frightened places of our hearts. Our child accepts us without reservation, a neighbor offers help when we were too proud to ask, a bank teller smiles with a word of grace after we've complained about a mistake that was ours all along—and we come face-to-face with Jesus.

But then there are the other times, the days when our view of Jesus seems obstructed by the crowd, when undesirable people or difficult situations obscure his presence. At those times we can barely make him out. Perhaps it is the insistent panhandler or the unruly student, the struggling co-worker or the needy client. But then again, could it be that there is more there than at first it seemed? If we want to catch sight of Jesus, we must be willing to look beneath the surface, to uncover the reality of his presence concealed behind the obvious and the ordinary. And there he is . . . hidden Jesus.

Coming to see Christ in each other, in all the obvious *and* in all the hidden places, lays bare the heart of joy. Our common moments are made uncommon with his presence, our regular routine carries the touch of the divine, our average day intersects eternity. Seeing Jesus happens not in avoiding those dry and dusty times or evading those people who get in the way but in learning to sift through it all to find the Jesus who was always there. For then, even when our lives are rattled or our daily grind is as routine as it gets, we can know that the delight of our days, the One whose compassion can quench our thirsty soul, is just beneath the surface if we'll only look more closely and learn to identify him.

Look closer. You might not see him at first, but he's there, in the same place Zacchaeus found him: in the press of the crowd, among the people who populated his town and filled his day. That's where we, too, come face-to-face with Jesus and encounter him: in our neighbors, in our friends, in the community of believers, at the local mall, in the fast-food guy who serves us lunch. Jesus stops and calls our name, saying, "Come down, I'm going to your house. For today salvation has come. . . ."

Some Things to Think About

1. What do you think it would have been like to meet Jesus face-to-face?

2. Imagine the moment when Zaccheaus first realized that Jesus had seen him. How do you think he felt? What do you think might have been going through his mind?

3. Where is the least expected place you have ever met Jesus?

4. What are the things/situations/people in your life that most easily or consistently blur your view of Jesus? How might you go about better identifying Jesus in those things/situations/people?

5. Describe a time when you felt Jesus' presence in what another person did for you.

6. Think of one person in whom you have trouble seeing Jesus. Look closer. How might this person be making Jesus more real for you?

chapter nine

When Push Comes to Shove

[The boy's father said] " . . . if you can do any-thing, take pity on us and help us."

"'If you can'?" said Jesus. "Everything is pos-sible for him who believes."

Immediately the boy's father exclaimed, "I do believe; help me overcome my unbelief!" (Mark 9:22-24)

I have issues with Jesus. He gets under my skin, asking me to do things that make me uncomfortable, such as caring about people I don't want to care about, forgiving people I don't want to forgive, giving up what I'd rather keep, dying to myself when I'd rather live for myself, serving when I'd much prefer to be served. Jesus asks me to believe things that are difficult to believe, with absolutely no hard evidence to make the believing any easier. Jesus wants me to trust him when I can't even see him; he asks me to take risks for him when I'd rather find comfort for myself. He invites me to cling to hope when I more naturally wallow in despair.

I have issues with Jesus.

One of my biggest issues is why he doles out miracles to some people like a congressman ladles out election-year pork, but, like some stingy kid who won't share his candy, he withholds those same miracles from others who have prayed just as hard, whose faith has been just as determined. Now, if you've been a recipient of a miracle—and I know there are some of you out there—I'm glad for you. Your story inspires me, your experience gives me hope, you have been blessed, and I am grateful for it and for you. Your miracle is a window into a world that is not yet, but someday will be.

But for everyone who gets a miracle, there seems to be thousands who do not, and a bunch of those people over the years have made their way to my office. With looks of hurt and confusion etched across their faces, they tell me how much they've prayed and nothing happened, how desperately they needed an answer and it didn't come, how deeply they believed and nothing seemed to change. And they wonder why. So do I.

Ron needed a miracle. I first met Ron when he appeared in my office unannounced, the day after he attended a class I was teaching on family relationships. After a quick introduction, Ron began to run down the litany of his problems. He used drugs. His marriage was ending. He'd abused his step-daughter and lost visitation rights with his son. He had no money, and he needed to make good on some bad checks. He had stolen a friend's gun and hawked it at the pawn shop.

Sooner or later, many such conversations like this have concluded with a request for financial assistance: If I could just spare a few dollars, it would help until they get could back on their feet. Ron's plea was even more basic: Would I take him to the hospital where he was going to check himself into drug rehab? But before we left, would I tell him about Jesus? He was trying to get his life straightened out, he said, and he figured this was the place to begin. He finished by explaining why he had come to my office: "I'm desperate. I've never sunk so low. I've got nowhere else to go. I've got nothing else. I'm reaching out."

The one thing Ron had carefully avoided for so long, through all the lies and bluster and self-deceit, he was finally confronting. There was nothing else that would work. There was nowhere else to turn. If Jesus couldn't help him, no one could. Ron knew he was facing his last, best hope for redemption, to become more than he was. When push came to shove, he finally realized there was nowhere else to go.

That fundamental truth must have been on the mind of the man whose story Mark records in chapter nine. This father, too, was desperate and needed a miracle. Not a moment had passed in all the years since his son's childhood that he had not agonized over the boy's plight. Each night tears flooded the man's eyes with an impotent grief; he could do nothing to help his son. Each morning dawned upon a renewed fear that this might be the day when his son's tragic condition would finally wrest away what little bit of life his son still had.

No doctor had been able to help. No miracle worker's mysterious incantations had spared his son from a single tormented moment. Nothing the man tried had relieved a single twitching muscle or kept his son's terrified eyes from rolling backward in his head. It was not a burning faith that brought this man to Jesus; it was a sense of utter futility, a lunging grab at a ragged shred of hope. He had heard of this Jesus, and he was determined to find him and ask him to do for his son what he, all these helpless years, had been unable to do. When push came to shove, he, too, had nowhere else to go; he had nothing left to lose. He had already lost his son years before.

I understand this man. Perhaps you do, too. The halting request stumbling from his mouth in the form of a last-ditch gamble articulates the frequent nature of faith: qualified, conditional, timid. Let's face it: Faith can be a messy, difficult, confusing affair. For most of us, it does not come easy. It is a rather fragile thing, arrived at in struggle, tested by turmoil; at one moment strong and vibrant, and the next, wobbling like a dingy in a sudden squall. Life charts a treacherous course among dangerous rocks and hidden shallows, amid the gale forces of daily challenges, and sometimes it is as much as we can do to hold onto the tattered edges of our belief. We find ourselves caught midway between faith and doubt. Not much joy there . . .

That's where the man in Mark's story found himself. Ron was in the same place, but for a different set of reasons. Standing amid the ruins of life, they both faced a reality that our busy, micro-managed lives can obscure: They were out of options. There was nowhere to go but to Jesus.

The fact is, desperation is often what pushes us most directly toward Christ. The rest of the time we tend to hedge our bets, thinking that we remain in control and we still have a range of choices available. As long as, to some degree, we think we can handle things on our own, we will likely try. The most fortunate among us recognize that when push comes to shove, we've got nowhere else to go.

It's not easy, at least for most of us. My faith would really "pop" if I could get me one of those miracles now and then. I confess, sometimes I want Jesus to act a little more like Zeus, hurling a miracle at me on occasion like a thunderbolt. Not all the time, just sometimes. Life would seem so much less ordinary, and faith so much less commonplace.

Clearly faith was not a simple matter for the boy's father, either. One word gave him away. It's a small word with a big meaning. Its two letters color everything that follows: *if*. "*If* you can do anything," said the man. Hardly a ringing statement of certainty. It doesn't make the short list of the most eloquent testimonies ever spoken. It sounds more like the realization of a man who has come face-to-face with his own powerlessness.

We often approach Jesus on an "if you can" basis. Instead of praying for healing, we resort to simply asking the Lord to "be with Uncle Ted." Rather than coming to Jesus bearing the specifics of our life, we pray in vague generalities: *if*. It isolates us from the risk of total trust. It cocoons God in a protective coating of theological principles so that when things don't go our way, we won't have to struggle with disturbing questions about God's faithfulness or our unmet expectations. When we pray for the tough things and God doesn't act as we expect or hope, we're left with puzzling doubts. So it seems easier to temper our faith with "if."

When we come to Jesus with an "if" on our lips, it's a clear signal that we've misplaced our trust. We've placed it in ourselves. Not in our own abilities, of course, but in the strength of our faith. "If" thinks faith is what makes miracles happen. We trust our faith in Jesus more than we trust Jesus, as though he will act only when we ratchet up our faith to the necessary levels. "If" assumes that the depth of our faith is the key ingredient in the work of Christ. "If you can" really comes to mean "if we believe," as though there were some sort of mathematical equation between our faith and God's response.

Faith is not a commodity we invest on an anticipated return. Faith is not something we do to demonstrate our readiness for a cure. Faith is a response to the mercy of our Savior. It is Jesus' love that ignites the spark, not our faith that prods Jesus into action. Jesus does not set conditions before we come to him, and grace does not depend on our efforts. "If" may be the destroyer of trust, but it is never the destroyer of Jesus' love.

"I believe," said the father, "but I know I don't believe enough. I know my faith is wavering and indecisive and fickle. Jesus, I don't know everything there is to know about you, but I do know my heart is breaking. I'm not even sure I believe you can do anything, or that you will choose to if you can, but I am sure that if there is any answer, if there is any hope for my precious son, it must be in you. Help my unbelief."

A simple, tentative cry from a desperate man. Jesus was his only answer.

That's faith. It's not very pretty at times. It may not be terribly inspiring to others, or even to ourselves. It may not be as strong as we'd like or move many mountains. But if it's all we have, it's all we need. The seedbed of faith is a recognition that nothing else will do, no other answer will satisfy, every other alternative fails, any other promise disappoints, and every other joy will fade. All other options are so much snake oil sold out of the back of a wagon by a humanity unable to trust anyone but themselves. But faith dares to look in a different direction, plagued by doubts and weak in the knees, yet banking on the promise that Jesus will help.

The desperate request, the qualified faith, the hope of belief tempered by the doubt of disbelief . . . it was enough for Jesus. It is always enough. In this face-to-face encounter, Jesus responded, not to the eloquence of the man's request nor the strength of his faith, but to the depth of his pain. It is never about the strength of our faith; it is never about the certainty of our belief; it is never about the level of our trust. With Jesus, it is always about the needs and the hurts and the hardships we bring.

And so, Jesus acted. He spoke the word, gave a command. And in a shrieking convulsion, the spirit was gone. Jesus restored the boy to his father. Jesus' love is more extravagant than any "if" that settles on our lips, his mercy stronger than the power of any hesitant faith, his compassion greater than our unbelief.

That's the fundamental reality that streaks joy across our daily struggles. Jesus makes all the difference for a present that would otherwise be uncertain. He heals past guilt that can stagger us without warning. He leads us on the way toward a tomorrow that already belongs to him. When push comes to shove, we have nowhere else to go for a love and acceptance that reaches beyond our feeble attempts at faith. Nowhere else to turn for a life that extends beyond the grave. Nowhere else to go for a hope that does not founder on the rocks of disappointment. Nowhere else to turn for a Savior whose patience can draw us beyond our "ifs."

I still have some issues with Jesus about this miracle thing because there are people I so desperately want to see him cure, in the way that I think they should be cured. But here's the real miracle: Jesus makes it possible for me to trust him anyway—though sometimes my faith is little more than a thick gruel of belief and unbelief. Jesus does not require that I be sure, but that I be honest. If all I have in me is the ability to come to him with my feeble "if you can," that is all I need. That is not only a big relief, it is a cause for joy because most of the time, in the course of my ordinary faith, I'm not able to whip up an acceptable level of certainty or a critical mass of faith. But I don't have to. All I have to do is come to Jesus, and he'll take care of the rest.

You probably want me to tell you that Ron got his miracle. To tell you the truth, I don't know what happened to Ron. Soon after we met, I moved to a different state and we lost touch. But I do know what happened to the man in Mark 9, and his son. Jesus healed the boy despite the wavering faith of his father. And I know this as well: Jesus offered himself to Ron. Just as he offers the strength of his grace to you, and to me. When push comes to shove, he's what we need. For life. For hope. For ordinary joy.

Some Things to Think About

1. What are some of your issues with Jesus?

2. On a scale from 1 to 10, with 1 being the lowest, how would you describe your faith level. Consider writing a letter or e-mail to Jesus telling him about your belief and your unbelief.

3. The author writes, "The fact is, desperation is often what pushes us most directly toward Christ. The rest of

the time we tend to hedge our bets . . ." In what ways might that be true or untrue for you?

4. Think of a time when you felt you had a problem and nowhere you could go for help. What help eventually made its way known to you? How do you see Jesus in this?

5. What do you see as the difference between relying on your faith and relying on Jesus? Would you agree with the idea that honesty about your faith is at least as important as certainty in your faith? Why?

6. In what way is the fact that we don't know what happened to Ron a fitting ending for this chapter?

part two

Serving God
in Ordinary Ways

chapter ten

Needing
to Be Needed

"Here is a boy with five small barley loaves and
two small fish, but how far will they go among so
many?" . . . Jesus then took the loaves . . .
(John 6:9, 11)

At the core of the human heart is the need to be needed.
One of our deepest human longings is to know that
we are ultimately important to someone. We want to
know that, without us, someone significant would be
missing. It's not that we think we're indispensable. We
don't always need to be the star. It's just that we want
to know we count. And we know we count when someone needs us.

I think of Helen. She sits alone in her wheelchair,
silently staring at nothing. Her eyes are sad, openings to
an inner spirit containing a profound emptiness. When-
ever I visit her, sooner or later she will say it: "I'm already
dead. Dead and buried."

Helen understands that, given her frail health, the
nursing home is where she must live. Still, she feels
robbed of something vital. She senses that she is no longer needed. Not by her children, though they visit her

regularly. Not by her church, though on occasion someone comes to call. Not by anyone. The world can live well without her. Though her body has betrayed her, her mind is sharp. The thing that is missing is the thing that makes life worthwhile: She needs to be needed.

Tim and Anne also come to mind. They sit across from each other in my office. They've decided it is time to face the reality of a struggling marriage. The conversation covers broad territory until it finally arrives at the real issue. "There was a time," Tim sighs, "when things were good. We laughed together. We enjoyed being with each other. I guess the paths we're on have taken us in different directions."

"We don't share much anymore," Anne volunteers. A tear escapes the corner of her eye, leaking pain onto her cheek. A shrug hunches Tim's shoulders. Both agree it wasn't supposed to be this way.

She whispers, "You don't love me anymore."

"Of course I do," he protests. "I tell you I love you every day."

"Yes, you do. You use the words. But you don't need me anymore. You are self-sufficient. I'm no longer a necessary part of your life. I need you to *need* me. That's how I know you mean it when you say you love me, because you still need me."

Then there was a young girl's father who reached down to tie his daughter's shoes.

"I can do it myself!"

Her demand was insistent as she pulled away. She spurned his offer of help with a determined pout. Finally, after starts and stops, mistakes, and bunny-eared loops that wouldn't stay put, she accomplished her task. She had tied her shoes.

A smile crossed her father's face, a surge of pride rushed through his heart. But he was surprised to feel an unexpected, small stab of pain buried in this moment. Here was another stage passed. Another thing his daughter could do for herself.

I am no longer that young father, and, as I write, it has now been one week since my daughter was married. I find myself wondering, have she and I reached the moment I feared, the day when this once little girl, whom I held in my arms and who, in another time, was so dependent upon me, will no longer need me at all?

Admittedly, there are times when we need a break from being needed, when the pressures build, the demands overwhelm; when the need presenting itself seems too great, the sacrifice too exhausting. Sometimes a break from being needed would be nice. There are times when we'd like to run away and hide. We might want nothing more than to say, "Leave me alone." It is possible to feel *too* needed. But chances are, after catching our breath, the desire to be meaningful to others makes itself known again. There are few feelings in life sweeter than knowing we are needed.

Have you ever paused to ponder, "I wonder if God needs me?" Have you ever considered, in the middle of your incredible need for God, that the most profound display of God's love may be that God has chosen to need you?

We think of God as self-sufficient; God is. We understand God as all powerful, able to do anything; God can. We confess belief in a God who is the beginning and end of all things, who, in the words of the Nicene Creed, is "the almighty, the maker of heaven and earth, of all that is seen and unseen." We know our need for God. We need God's grace. We need God's acceptance. We need God's presence. We need God's power and comfort, wisdom and strength. We need God's forgiveness. All that we are can be expressed in our need of God. But could it be that, of all the incredible aspects of God's love, the most amazing is that God chooses to need us?

The story of Jesus feeding the five thousand is, among other things, the story of God choosing to need us. The crowd was hungry. They had been with Jesus all day, and he was concerned that they hadn't had anything to eat. As he looked out over the gathering, Jesus saw people who needed food not only for their souls, but for their stomachs. There was no need too mundane for Jesus to care about, not even a growling stomach at dinnertime.

Jesus turned to his panicking disciples, whose only contribution to the situation was a quick estimate of the cash register receipt involved in feeding this many people. Then John, in recounting this event, provides a detail the other Gospel writers omit. There was a boy, unexceptional and easily missed (Matthew, Mark, and Luke don't even mention him) who provided five loaves of bread and two fish. That's all he did. That's all he had. Not much to feed five thousand hungry people. But in Jesus' hands, it was enough.

Jesus could have chosen to do things differently. He could have decided to rain down manna from the sky. After all, God had done that once before. Jesus might have caused fish to jump out of the lake and into people's laps. He could have fed them in a thousand different ways. But he didn't. He turned to a small boy with nothing much to offer in proportion to what was needed and used what the boy had to give.

There are two miracles in this story, one imbedded in the other. The smaller, less impressive miracle has to do with providing a buffet lunch for some famished followers. Do you see the other miracle? The truly amazing one? It is the wonder of Jesus choosing to need what an unknown boy had to give.

It is the shocking surprise of God's love that God chooses to need us. It is a love so real, so true, so deep that it expresses itself in a need for us. Think of it. The Creator chooses to need the created. The infinite places his most cherished gift in the hands of the finite. The Holy makes use of what the sinful have to offer. But that is, after all, how love becomes real, isn't it? That's what gives depth to a relationship and meaning to life: when someone needs us.

Jesus needed a boy with five loaves and two fish. No doubt the boy, if he had any sense at all, realized that what he had to give was insignificant. Perhaps it even embarrassed him to mention it, the need was so great and his gift so small. I know how he felt. Perhaps you have felt the same way. What we have to give, we think, isn't worth much. The desire is there but the resources are limited. We can see the urgency, but our talents, abilities, and available time add up to five puny loaves and two scrawny fish. Not much. Maybe not even worth mentioning.

There's more to notice in this story. The clue lies in what Jesus did *not* say. Jesus did not ask the boy for three fish, when two was all the boy had. Jesus did not ask why the boy brought only five loaves when Jesus wanted six. Not only does Jesus, in his love, choose to need us, he takes what we have to offer and makes it enough. Jesus asks that we give him all that we have, but not more than we have. Our responsibility is to hold nothing back.

There is someone who needs to be fed. Someone who needs our prayer. Someone who needs our support. Someone who needs to be reached. No need to apologize for what little we have to give. What we have is all Jesus needs. The privilege we have been given is to offer ordinary service for an extraordinary God.

God chose to need a young, single girl named Mary to bear Embodied Love into the world. He chose to need a foreigner to carry his Son's heavy cross. Jesus chose to need a boy with a bit of bread and a pair of fish to feed five thousand people. And God chooses to need you.

That's the nature of God's love. He knows you need to be needed. And so you are. Needed in the midst of your own need. Needed despite the tiny amount you have to contribute. Needed in your most ordinary days, in your most routine life. Needed by the very God who gave you life. Never underestimate what God can accomplish through what you have to share. You have a reason to sing; you have a reason to shout. God needs you.

And that is a source of joy!

Some Things to Think About

1. Who are the people you need in your life? Who needs you?

2. Think of a time in your life when you felt unneeded. How did you feel? Think of a time when you felt especially needed. Describe the differences in how you felt in each of those situations.

3. What do you think of the idea that God needs you? How might God's choosing to need you be an example of grace?

4. When you think of serving God, what are the things you think you have to offer? What feels like "not enough"? In what ways has God stretched your limited resources beyond what you thought you could give?

5. Think of some way you might reach out to a person in need in the next twenty-four hours.

6. Write a prayer expressing your need for God. Include thanks for God's need for you.

chapter eleven

One Thing I Know

"One thing I do know. I was blind, but now I
see!" (John 9:25)

In all of the Gospels, one of the most remarkable
witnesses to Jesus comes from a man who was completely confused. Neither a gifted theologian nor a
trained scholar, he was repeatedly questioned about
Jesus. In response he offered no dissertations about
the juxtaposition of the divine and human natures of
Christ. He cited no verses from the Torah or the Proph-
ets to undergird an apologetic argument. He did not
launch into a lecture on the relationship between grace
and faith. Most of his answers were tentative; much of
what he said showed him to be clearly out of his league
when it came to theological discussions. He displayed
no oratorical skills, he won few debating points, and
his thoughts were neither deep nor profound. So, how
was it this man, an ordinary, blind beggar, managed to
provide a witness to Jesus more powerful than a library
full of theological tomes?

John tells the man's story in chapter nine. Any chance at a productive life, any dreams that things could ever be different for this man were shuttered and locked away behind useless eyes. A lifetime of blindness consigned him to a lifetime of begging, for there was nothing else a sightless man could do. Sitting along the side of the road, endlessly waiting for someone to drop a coin in the rag beside his feet or press a bit of bread into his perpetually outstretched hand, he was the local theological object lesson. Well-intentioned people, their own insight as limited as this man's eyes, could only speculate at what crime he, or his parents, had committed that he should receive such a divine rebuke. Even Jesus' disciples thought the darkness of his world was a sure sign pointing to the sinfulness of his, or someone's, heart.

But that was before strong arms lifted him to his feet and rough hands rubbed mud on his eyes. That was before a voice he did not recognize cut through the hum of a crowded street, commanding him with a quiet authority to go and wash at the pool called "Sent." And as the mud slid away, a brightness he had never witnessed sparkled off the water and pierced his newly healed eyes. All around him moved shapes and colors and objects for which he had no words, for he had never seen them before. Until now.

When his neighbors wanted to know what on earth had happened, the formerly blind man simply told his story. He didn't embellish it, he didn't explain it; he simply shared it.

Ironically, his neighbors, with their ability to see, were unable to perceive what was so clear to the blind man. They wanted big answers to little questions, so they hauled him to an audience with the local religious experts, the Pharisees. The Pharisees asked the man what happened, and he told his story again. Not liking what they heard, the Pharisees turned to the man's parents.

"Tell us what this is all about," the Pharisees demanded.

The parents weren't much help. "How should we know? Ask our son."

The blind man was brought in yet another time. The Pharisees wanted answers: What happened? How did it happen? Who did this?

Read closely and you can almost hear the sarcasm welling up in the man's throat and dripping from his words: "Look, I told you once. Why do you want to hear it again? So you can become his disciples, too?"

With no answers to fit their tastes, the Pharisees fell back on their only remaining option: discredit the witness. "Why should we listen to you? You were born in sin anyway." And with that, the once-blind man was bounced from the temple. In the end, the person who had been unable to see was now the only one who could see clearly, while those who had boasted of their ability to see and understand everything ended up stubbornly determined to preserve their own blindness.

In all the exchanges that took place between the healed blind man and the people who questioned him, five key words keep popping up: "One thing I do know." They are easy to miss, for they seem rather ordinary and insignificant. They are words that could easily get lost, but they are worth spending a little time with.

While the Pharisees and neighbors sought to deny what their eyes told them, the man who had been blind struggled to see who Jesus really was. He could not answer their questions, but he knew Jesus had healed him. That was enough. The result was a powerful witness beginning with these five seemingly unimportant words: "One thing I do know."

"I don't know how he did it," said the newly seeing blind man, "but one thing I do know: I was blind but now I see."

"I don't know whether he is good or bad, but one thing I do know: He gave me sight."

"I don't know if he is the Messiah; I don't even know

what that means. One thing I do know: He opened my eyes and banished the eternal night in which I lived."

One thing I do know. That's the difference between darkness and light. It's what distinguishes a blind man who can see from sighted people who are blind. It's what separates ordinary existence from joy-filled living. It's the hook on which we hang our faith. The blind man's answers were clear and simple because he caught sight of something no one else recognized. "All I know is what he's done for me: He made me see."

One thing I do know. There is no more powerful witness than those five words. There is no more profound message. Those words are all we need for our witness to be effective. You say you don't know your Bible from cover to cover? That doesn't have to stop you from being a witness. You're intimidated because you don't have all the answers to every conceivable question someone might ask? Neither did the blind man, but it didn't slow him down. He had a story to tell, which only he could. He was the expert on what Jesus had done in his life. You are the expert on what Jesus has done in yours. By following this blind man's lead, you have the opportunity to share your faith on the basis of your own ordinary experience.

Allow me to explain by telling you about Jim. Until the evening he sat beside me in my living room, it seemed as if life had chosen to give Jim an extra portion of all the best it had to offer. He had a wife who loved him and a child whose beauty made the angels smile. They lived in a comfortable home, drove a nice car, worked at successful careers, and enjoyed the company of good friends. Jim had it all, and more, for he was fortunate enough to realize how good life was.

Then, one day, his wife announced that she was leaving. It wasn't another man, she said. It wasn't Jim's fault either; it was hers. She thought she needed to find herself, and so she left. And so Jim was sitting in my living room realizing for the first time that, for all he had, he didn't have what he needed most.

Jim was trying to tap into the personal strength on which he had always relied, but his strength that night was fragile. He spoke of how he would have to raise his daughter alone, and how he wanted his daughter grounded in something meaningful and deep, something he didn't have. Jim was looking for a resource that could get him through the hurt, a hope that existed on the other side of pain. He had tried some new age philosophies, but they had left him empty. Could it be, he wondered, that the faith he had rejected so long ago— and the Jesus he had long since forgotten—were what he needed?

We talked late into the night about the love I knew God had for Jim. How did I know, Jim asked. Because I have felt God's love in my life, I said. Because God has welcomed me home after I've wandered far too long. Because I can feel the joy of God's presence coursing through my spirit when I am near him, and I know the heaviness of its absence when I leave. No profound proofs. No unassailable arguments. Just my story of what Jesus was up to in my life.

I saw Jim for a while following that night, but he never again mentioned his search for meaning until a few years later when I received a Christmas card from him. Tucked inside was a note: Jim had found a church. He was involved in a Bible study. His hope was strong; his life was healing. And most of all he had found a Savior or, more accurately, the Savior had found him. He couldn't stop talking about it. He knew he had a lot to learn, he wrote, but he was making it a habit to tell everyone he knew about the Jesus he was getting to know.

Our lives and faith are filled with questions, many of them difficult and not easily answered. I don't know, for example, why there is suffering in the world, and sometimes I wonder why God doesn't do more about it. After years of seminary training and pastoral ministry, I still don't understand why some people pray for recovery and get well, while others pray just as urgently and yet die. I don't know why some people seem to have more luck than they know what to do with, while others seem to struggle through one crisis after another.

But one thing I do know: Jesus soothes the hurts that throb inside me. He is fine-tuned to my fears and hopes, my anger and love, my disappointments and delights, my sorrow and joy that all mix together in the complex stew that defines who I am. Jesus knows the darkness through which I walk. The touch of his hand on my heart brings a peace and healing I find nowhere else. There are many things I don't know, but one thing I do know: I have felt Jesus' compassionate presence in my life.

The most powerful witness we have, the strongest gift that is ours to share, is our own story. When people want to discover meaning in their lives and meet a Savior who will make a difference in their days, the towering example of a religious superstar is not likely to offer much practical help. It seems an unattainable goal, out of touch with their reality. You see, more than simply looking for answers, people want to meet Jesus. More than needing a theological fact sheet, they want to know a person. Often their most real encounter with him is through the story of our faith. It is seeing how Jesus' promises work themselves out in the common routines of life that will enflesh the God they seek.

Perhaps your faith feels anything but inspirational. Maybe your story underwhelms. I've run into that before. Every year, during the weeks of Lent leading up to Easter, our congregation gathers for midweek worship. There is never a sermon. There is no exposition of the Bible. As a preacher, it pains me to admit it, but maybe that is why so many people turn out. What each service contains is something we call a "Faith Story" in which a member of the congregation shares the story of where they have seen God in their life. Over the years people have told stories that have ranged from the dramatic and stirring to the standard and routine. One common thread that has weaved its way through story after story is the response I receive when I first ask if they will tell it. Universally, the reaction is one of surprise, mixed with a little embarrassment. "No one wants to hear my story," they say. "There isn't much to tell. It's not very interesting." My answer is always the same: "This is a story people need to hear because your story will remind them of their own. If they can discover God in your story, they're more likely to find God in theirs."

Recognizing God in our life is what joy is all about. The closer we get to Jesus, the more intensely we live all of those common moments that form the central core of who we are. The blind man's story teaches us that it is not what we know about Jesus that is crucial; it is the Jesus we know who makes the difference. Understanding what we believe is important, but when we allow ourselves to be intimidated by what we don't know, our hearts may remain unaffected by the One whose touch can restore and remake us. Sharing the God we have met—as simple as that story may be—is the spigot that releases joy.

Take one more look at the blind man's story. Something far more profound happened than a man receiving his sight. His life took on new shape. Notice how his response changed as the story moved forward. When his neighbors wanted to know how it happened, the man responded by simply telling the story. When the religious leaders wanted to know what he thought of the man who healed him, he said Jesus was a prophet. As the story moved along, the formerly blind man became more convinced that the One who healed him was from God. Finally, Jesus asked the man if he believed in the Son of Man, and when Jesus revealed himself, the man responded by saying, "I believe in you."

Do you see the progression? Each time the man was challenged to give an account of what had happened to him, he became more convinced of what he believed. His witness progressed from referring to Jesus as a man, to confessing Jesus as Lord. That is the nature of faith: The more we share it, the more it grows.

One thing I do know. These are powerful words of witness containing the story of Jesus in our lives. And they are available to anyone—to you—who has known the touch of Jesus upon their eyes or upon their heart.

Some Things to Think About

1. What is your experience of Jesus in your life? When have you particularly felt Jesus' touch?

2. Reflect on the following statement: "The closer we get to Jesus, the more intensely we live all of those common moments that form the central core of who we are." In what way do you agree or disagree with that thought?

3. What are some of the bedrock things you know to be true about Jesus, based on your personal experience? How does knowing those things contribute to your sense of joy?

4. How do you react to the distinction between knowing *about* Jesus and knowing *Jesus?*

5. Try writing out the story of your faith, or telling it to someone this week. Note what was difficult about it. How did it give you joy?

6. When was the last time you told someone about your experience of Jesus? How did your sharing affect your faith?

chapter twelve

Thief of the Heart

> After this, Jesus traveled about from one town and village to another, proclaiming the good news of God. The Twelve were with him, and also some women who had been cured of evil spirits and diseases. . . . These women were helping to support them out of their own means. (Luke 8:1-3)

Barbie and I went on our first date together at the end of September. During the next month, my car broke down (I was a student and it was a heap), so I used hers (she worked full time and it was brand new). We lived on opposite sides of Minneapolis; she lived south and I lived north. To get to school in St. Paul, I had to drive east, and I worked evenings in a western Minneapolis suburb. Get the picture? Each day I followed a torturous route, crisscrossing the city from north to east to west. But each night, before I drove north to go home, I first drove south to see Barbie. I probably could have skipped that extra trip now and then, but I never did; I didn't want a day to go by without seeing her (and besides . . . it was her car). We do some unexpected things when we lose our hearts to someone. . . .

One month after our first date, I asked Barbie to marry me. (No, it had nothing to do with saving on gasoline costs!) We told everyone, however, that we had been see-ing each other six weeks. At the time we thought that sounded more respectable. That was October. In picking a wedding date, I employed some very precise logic. I reasoned that if we set a June date, we would just get impatient and move it up. Better, so my thinking went, to pick the earlier date to begin with. Barbie bought it and I rejoiced, and by February's end we were married. (If my children did something like that, I'd be horrified!)

When someone loves us and we lose our heart to them, their love calls forth our love. Their passion initi-ates actions and responses that weren't present before. Their love causes us to behave in ways we might not even consider normal or wise. Love invites us to make sacrifices and not count them as such. That's the nature of love. That's the fire that passion kindles.

When we lose our hearts to someone who can call forth the best in us, who is gentle and tender with us as no one else has ever been, it affects us so deeply, it is as if nothing else matters. When someone steals our heart and fills us with love and value, hope and joy, our life is changed. Nothing is ever the same. Their love creates love in us.

Mary would tell you. So would Joanna. Susanna would back them up. They knew firsthand, for they apparently each lost their heart to Jesus. We don't know what role Jesus played in Susanna's life; this is the only place in the New Testament where she is mentioned by name. Joanna must have sacrificed her role as the manager of a household, for we are told that she was the wife of Herod's business manager. And Mary . . . the day would come when Jesus would show himself alive after she had seen him sag, dead, upon a cross. But at the moment, as Luke formally introduces her in chapter eight, he tells us that Jesus had cast out seven demons from her. The one thing all three women had in common was that Jesus had cured them of evil spirits and diseases, and as a result they, along with his disciples, accompanied him on his travels and helped to support him in his itinerant ministry. In healing them, Jesus had communicated his love and compassion. In releasing them from harassing spirits, Jesus had claimed their hearts. It is little wonder, then, that these three, and others like them, ordinary people with homes and lives and jobs, had set off after Jesus, the One to whom they'd given their hearts.

What a joy it is to be loved. What an awesome, tremendous thing it is to be cherished. As a child, I knew how important I was when my father would tuck me into bed at night. Some nights he would sing to me. Now, my dad couldn't carry a tune any better than I could dribble a basketball down a court and dunk it through the hoop—which is to say, not at all. Most people have never heard my dad sing in public. But as he pulled the blankets up, he would lean on the edge of my bed and sing "Old Shep." In the dusky twilight my father would sing about a boy and his dog, and I knew I was cherished. As an adult, I still have a Father who sings: My Father God sang my life into existence, and in his Son, Jesus, God sings to life the love in my heart.

Do you know the deep satisfaction of being treasured? Have you ever experienced a time, even a moment, when someone so totally cared for you that you knew you were beloved?

Perhaps you have known it in your marriage, and though sometimes you forget, there are still those times when you are wide-eyed with wonder that someone could know you so well and adore you so much.

Perhaps you experienced love as a child when your parents let you know that you were more important to them than their own desires. And now, as a parent yourself, you long to impart those same feelings to your kids, though your temper is sometimes short and your frustrations long.

I have a friend whose name is Merle. Our friendship goes back years, to my college days. Merle was the best man at my wedding. Merle and his wife still live in Minnesota, but Merle comes to Southern California, where I live, on business from time to time. The other afternoon he called from the airport to tell me he was in the area and asked about my schedule. I explained to him that both Barbie and I had a 7 P.M. meeting. "Well that would work," he said. He would just drive up from the airport . . . at 4 P.M., a time of day in L. A. when driving the freeway is about as enjoyable as pulling out your own teeth. We could maybe meet for dinner for an hour or two, and then we'd both go our way. Merle is persistent in his friendship, willing to make a seventy-mile round trip at rush hour just for the chance to have some time together. It's what Merle does to let me know he values our friendship and cares about me.

Maybe a friend has let you know you are loved. Some-one who stayed with you when you were confused and tried to push people away. Someone who took the brunt of your misplaced anger and bore the pain of your self-inflicted wounds. Someone who would not give up on you, even when the relationship was strained. Someone who was the anchor in your storm. Knowing yourself to be treasured by another person is a gift that comes in an endless variety of wrappings.

Or perhaps you have never known the feeling of being someone's beloved. Somewhere along the line, the person you counted on to love you let you down. Maybe you have been cared for but never cherished, known security but never been prized. Maybe you learned how to be tough because no one ever cried for you. Perhaps you have a spouse, a family, parents, and a dog, but you don't know what it's like to be adored.

There is One in whose eyes you are precious. To him, you are worth more than life itself. His love never wanes, never withdraws. Jesus never takes you for granted. He will never treat your love with callous indifference. If you know the tenderness Jesus has for you in his heart, you've lost your heart to him, just as Mary, Joanna, and Susanna did.

Following Jesus is not a duty but a delight. It's not an obligation but an opportunity. It has little to do with gritty determination, for true discipleship, as in true love, is about responding to the one who cherishes us. The three women, and others like them, didn't follow Jesus because he demanded it; they responded out of an awareness of having been rescued by him. Jesus doesn't say we *must* be disciples. He never commands us to give more, participate more, grow more, sacrifice more, do more. He invites us to lose ourselves in his love. The unrestrained nature of his love captivates our hearts. His unwavering passion for us creates a response within us. And it changes everything. As with any relationship of love, it compels us to live beyond ourselves and respond to the love we've received.

We all know what kinds of things love causes us to do. When we lose our heart to someone who loves us, we plunge ourselves into that relationship with little consideration as to whether we are acting sensibly, meeting the standards of others, or looking foolish. None of that matters. The only thing that counts is our beloved. Deep love is not by nature a carefully controlled, even-tempered emotion. It is most definitely not a cerebral event in which we coldly analyze the ramifications of our actions. It is a hot rush of desire to be with this person at any cost, to throw caution to the wind because we feel this person completes us, to reserve no part of ourselves from this relationship. And that is exactly the basis—and no other—on which we follow and serve Jesus; not because we must, but because we lose our heart to him.

Jesus loves us the way we really are. He did not love Mary Magdalene only after she was demon-free and had washed herself clean. His love set her free. He did not heal Joanna or Susanna only when they promised to support his ministry. He healed them first and then they followed. Peter denied him the night he was arrested. Thomas doubted him when he appeared after Easter. All the disciples deserted him when, at the cross, he needed them most. And yet in each case, Jesus' love restored them. Examine the Gospels: Like riders crammed in a rush-hour subway, goodness and evil jostle each other on every page. There are good people with fatal flaws, and flawed people that somehow get things right. The Gospels are populated with well-intentioned folk who never quite live completely up to their grand plans. We're introduced to fickle people who encounter Christ one minute and forget him the next, and faithful people who struggle to trust promises that seem too incredible to believe. There are leaders who won't lead, followers who won't follow, lusty men, iron-willed women, people who know how to love, and people whose hatreds refuse to subside. And without exception, Jesus loved every one of them. Perhaps that's what was on the Apostle Paul's mind when he called attention to our status as "dearly loved children," people whom Christ loved and gave himself up for (Ephesians 5:1-2).

When my children were younger, we would take driving trips back to Minnesota to see our relatives. The best part of it, for me, was the time we spent together as a family. Everyday life has an insidious way of robbing families of the simple pleasure of being with each other. Our family was no different. Agendas and commitments, responsibilities and competing priorities shouldered their way into our days, crowding out time for those we loved the most. But vacation brought us back together again, huddled in a camper around a single light, playing games, telling silly jokes, and laughing together. At those moments I was reminded: These are my beloved children. Sometimes I don't think they comprehend how incredibly important they are to me. Sometimes it surprises me how much I love them and how deeply that love runs. Sometimes it overwhelms me.

And sometimes I think we do not comprehend our status as children of God whose love put on skin and came to us in Jesus Christ. This is a love that wants nothing more than to reach out and bring us near when we are distant. It is a love so totally taken with us that, like a swimmer in the deepest lake, we can't touch the bottom of it. When we are loved with that kind of passion and abandon, when we are loved as no other loves us, when we are loved with a wild recklessness that nothing we do can derail, that is the foundation for joyful living and joyful serving. Like water that seeps into every crack, that fills every fissure, that runs into every depression, the love of God in Christ, when we let it fully into our lives, saturates the empty places and fills in the missing spaces.

When we, in turn, lose our hearts to this Lover of our souls, something happens within us. God's love becomes a pattern for our own. We become, as Paul describes, imitators of God (Ephesians 5:1).

When I was in junior high, Mr. Valsvic's job was to teach me industrial arts, but he mostly intimidated me. I am a proud member of that category of male known as the handiwork challenged. We are the ones able to walk right down the center aisle in the hardware store without so much as a blip in our testosterone level. But I was in seventh grade and industrial arts was required, and Mr. Valsvic was supposed to teach me.

He tried.

Mr. Valsvic taught by telling. He followed the principle that if he explained what he wanted us to do, we would then be able to perform the necessary tasks to accomplish the project. My handle-less cookie cutters argued otherwise. My tool box with its top welded on backward suggested I hadn't quite caught the idea. The burned-out electrical panel at our work station seemed to indicate that telling me what to do didn't necessarily guarantee that I could do it. Insistent commands went head-to-head with lack of talent. Disinterest on the battlefield of shop class and lack of talent won a lopsided victory.

My dad used a different technique for teaching. Growing up in Minnesota where winter streets were stained white with salt, and buying a new car was the stuff of a high school boy's daydreams, fixing the rusted bodies of older model cars became a dependable signal that summer had arrived. My first car was a '62 Chevy that reminded me of the undead in a grade B horror movie. Technically, it was still running, but its body was rapidly falling apart. To postpone its final gasp yet one more year meant that I would have to scrape and sand the fenders, and ladle on copious amounts of body putty. That, too, would require sanding and then painting. My industrial arts experiences indicated I should not get my hopes up.

My father instructed me to take the sander in my hands, then placing his hands around mine, he swirled the sander in the circular motion that good sanding requires. When it was time to paint, I would have drained the spray gun in a single swipe, thinking that if a little paint is good, a lot of paint is better, and all at once saves work. Instead, Dad handed me the gun and once again, putting his hands around mine, together we applied the lightest of first coats. The final result was a car that no longer looked like it had seen better days.

Mr. Valsvic taught me because it was his job, and he was paid to endure a year of my bizarrely lopsided and ridiculously strange projects. But my dad . . . he loved me. And the way he taught me showed me that. He gave me a pattern, something to imitate. I'll never be as good as my dad at sanding and painting and restoring something that is broken, but because he taught me with hands of love, I understand the touch, I know the feel of what he does and what I am to do.

Jesus, too, teaches by modeling. He wants us to love, so first he loves us. In Jesus, God wraps gentle hands around ours and teaches us what it is like to be loved, what it means to live as God's people. God guides and shapes what we do. We live our lives in the Father's touch, in the embrace of God's love, wrapped in grace, with God's heart beating the rhythm of love into our days.

Paul suggests that our status as beloved children allows us to follow the pattern of love set down in Christ. In doing so, we discover the building blocks of joyful living and meaningful serving. Our deepest joys come in loving and being loved.

In the end, Mary, Joanna, and Susanna discovered love's amazing truth: Encountering Jesus means losing your heart to him. And this thief of the heart is looking for yours.

Some Things to Think About

1. Think of a time when you "fell in love." What was that experience like? What did you do that you might not have done under ordinary circumstances?

2. Think of someone who loves you. In what ways are you precious to them? How do they let you know that?

3. Think of someone who taught you by "modeling" rather than by "telling." How did that affect your ability to learn from them?

4. How do you experience the love of Jesus? In what way does your response to his love impact your life, the choices you make?

5. What are some ways in which you are tempted to retain the keys to your heart rather than give it to Jesus? How does that impact the joy in your faith life?

6. How would you describe the difference between believing in God and loving Jesus with wild abandon? Which characterizes your life of faith?

chapter thirteen

Divine Interruptions

A certain man from Cyrene, Simon, the father of
Alexander and Rufus, was passing by on his way
in from the country, and they forced him to carry
the cross. (Mark 15:21)

Simon of Cyrene rates but a single verse in Matthew,
Mark, and Luke, and he is not mentioned at all in John.
Given the task he performed—carrying Jesus' cross—one
might think the Gospel writers would supply a bit more
information. Who was Simon? What did he look like?
What did he think when he was pressed into service? Did
Jesus say anything to him as the harsh splinters from the
rough wood bit into Simon's shoulder? Or did Simon drag
the cross in silence up the slopes of Calvary, unaware of
the part he was playing in the salvation of the world? The
Evangelists offer nothing but a simple reference. They do
not praise him, nor follow his story. It would appear that
there was no glamour in the task Simon performed. But
perhaps the outcome was joy. Maybe that's the way it is
when one becomes a servant.

Biblical scholars suggest that Simon was likely a
Jewish pilgrim attending Passover in Jerusalem. He no

doubt had traveled long and difficult miles, having come from Cyrene, in North Africa. Considering the distance, this may have been his first Passover in the Holy City. Chances are this was something for which he had planned and saved and spent years anticipating. Finally, he had arrived. Like any tourist, Simon would have been ready with his day's agenda, the places he would go, the things he would do, the sites he would see. What he was not prepared for was running into a grisly parade of soldiers and convicts.

Nor could he have been pleased with the next interruption in his busy day. In the wrong place at the wrong time, Simon felt a tap on his shoulder and, before he knew it, he was carrying a cross. That is one thing the Gospels make clear: Simon did *not* volunteer. He had not planned on this intrusion into his busy day. He was not inclined toward the humiliation of transporting a criminal's cross in front of a jeering crowd to the site of Jesus' execution. But a pack of Roman soldiers had a different idea. So did God.

Simon's situation has a ring of familiarity about it. There are times when servanthood is no easy task. We are called to serve. We've heard it from the pulpit; we've read it in the Bible. We know Jesus' words about being a servant; we know he washed the feet of his disciples and told us to do the same.

The desire to serve is rooted in our hearts; the need to serve grows within us. The problem is not lack of motivation; it's much more mundane than that. The dilemma servanthood raises is that most often the call to serve is inconvenient. It comes unexpectedly and unplanned for in a legitimately busy week. The needs of others burst in upon us, refusing to be slated for an appropriate time. We labor day in and day out under the pressure of an agenda, a set of priorities and responsibilities rigid in their unwillingness to be compromised. To pause in service is to face interruptions in a demanding schedule and risk the possibility that our own needs, and the very important things we are doing at that moment, will go ignored.

The tyranny of daily living bends our attention inward on ourselves. Ever watch a sunflower develop? I spent a summer living on a farm in South Dakota, and I noticed something about the fields of sunflowers that greeted me in every direction. They are a study in the way our lives are constructed. As a young plant, in the spring of the year, a sunflower shoots up to ever increasing heights. It flowers a brilliant yellow, shining with all the rich beauty of its namesake. Each day it faithfully turns its face to the sun and tracks the sun's progress across the sky.

As the summer wears on, something begins to change. The seeds in that flower begin to grow, and the developing fruit brings with it an ironic fate. Late in the season, it takes on a heaviness that twists and tugs at the flower, sagging the plant's stalk until it curves toward the ground. The once radiant sunflower no longer turns toward the sun; it simply droops under the weight of the fruit, its head bent low and weary.

Sound familiar? Sometimes ordinary life nearly compels us to self-centeredness. The very blessings we crave seem to ratchet our perspective into increasing preoccupation with how to keep what we have, generate more, and make ends meet. The demands of the job control our time, our children's activities set our schedules, what we want morphs into what we need. Instead of following the Son, we double over from the weight of the good life until all we can see is the impact another interruption will have on an over-stressed day. Life loses something when its central focus is down and in, rather than up and out.

Complicating matters, the person who most needs our care is often the person we find the most distasteful. The power of their need can act like a suction cup on the soul, threatening to drain it dry. There isn't a person reading this book who hasn't been confronted by someone seeking help, and it's not always limited to those you run into on the street. There is always someone in need: a neighbor, a friend, a co-worker. An acquaintance or a family member, a church member, or even a stranger needs your time, the most precious commodity you have, because you have so little of it. When you say "no," you may feel guilty. When you say "yes," you may feel resentful.

If life teaches us that we ought to be the subject of our own attention, servanthood tugs us in a decidedly opposite direction, smudging the line between acting in humility and feeling humiliated, between giving of ourselves and feeling used. The feeling that following Jesus translates into being constantly available to others can wring the joy from service until it becomes a resented obligation. As Simon of Cyrene could tell us, the problem with Jesus is that he insists on showing up in the wrong people, at all the wrong times.

Jesus' call to servanthood rings loud and inviting in the hearing, but in the course of ordinary life, it can be hard in the doing. I discovered that with a young man named Todd. I did not want to serve Todd, and he knew it. I was working in a residential facility for physically disabled young adults where Todd lived. I was an orderly, and my job was to care for the needs of the residents. I was to help them with their personal hygiene, assist them at dinner, aid them in getting changed and into bed for the night. Most times I did it cheerfully.

But Todd made it difficult. I seriously considered handing in my resignation on the spot every time I was assigned to him. Todd had a way of making me painfully aware that I was serving him. Most residents were grateful for the help the staff provided, considerate and polite in their requests, regarding us as their friends. Todd was different. Todd made a point of asking for help when he could clearly see I was overloaded with other responsibilities. Invariably, he would decide to go to bed—a task that easily demanded an hour—fifteen minutes before a shift change. The rest of the staff were out watching TV with the residents, waiting to punch out for the night. But, with the reliability of an alarm clock, I would hear the whirring of Todd's electric wheelchair cruising the hallway as he looked for me to put him to bed. I took to hiding in the linen closet.

Todd challenged me to serve him. He wanted his shoes in a certain place, his clothes hung in a particular fashion, and pillows placed behind his back in exacting locations. Todd wore a beard, and there was always something in that beard, something that didn't belong there. But Todd was quadriplegic and could not remove it himself, so it fell to me to deal with the offending food.

It was not only the challenge, nor the way Todd's demands interfered with my other duties and plans that bothered me. It was that Todd enjoyed my serving him. He enjoyed it entirely too much, in my opinion, and I did not find it a pleasant task. It felt, instead, demeaning. It chipped away at my young man's pride. Rather than entering into Todd's life, I wanted to serve him while remaining distant, aloof, and in control. But Todd insisted I serve him on his terms, not mine, and his constant challenge called into question my self-perceptions. So I did not want to serve him at all.

In my inability to serve Todd, there was one thing I missed. I missed the opportunity to draw close to my Lord. We are never without a chance, even in the most mundane moments of our ordinary lives, to love and be loved by the One whose cross we are invited to carry.

To be a servant freely and joyfully, we must begin by identifying ourselves as among those who have been served. It is not until we recognize the extent to which Jesus has met our deepest needs that we will be free to willingly serve him as he appears to us in others.

In that sense we have something in common with Simon of Cyrene. The Man for whom Simon carried the cross was the One whose death would save him. Though Simon was unaware of the implications of what would soon take place on the cross he bore, the crucifixion would make possible for Simon to be released from his sin and the death that accompanied it. Ultimately, the One whom Simon was serving was the One who was serving him.

When I realize that all the callousness, all the self-involvement, all the unwillingness to love that I find so ugly in society exists within me, then I know I am as in need as those to whom I am called to minister. It is not "they" who need help, it is I. I am the one whose sin required a cross. I am the one whose feet have been washed by a serving Savior, whose bleating lostness brought the Shepherd in search, whose splintered spirit is healed again and again by his touch.

Think about this: Jesus spent his time with individuals. Though he preached to crowds, and large groups sought him out, nearly all his miracles took place for individual people, people with a particular hurt, people engaged in the challenge of ordinary living. He provided wine for a worried host at his daughter's wedding. He restored a son to his grief-stricken mother. He healed a woman who, after countless doctor visits, still could find no relief. Rather than being an interference in his crowded schedule, each person was worth his attention. For Jesus, interruptions were openings for ministry, distractions were occasions to share love, disturbances were healing, life-giving moments.

The key to a life of service is to be open to the moment, to recognize interruptions as divine appointments. Opportunities for caring occur in the ordinary circumstances of daily life. Consider the kid down the street—you know the one. Like sandwich wrap, he smothers you with a constant, clinging presence. Whether you like it or not, God has brought him into your life. Can you be his servant? What about the young man at church whose wife just left him—do you have a moment to call? The boss whose arrogance masks a fierce loneliness—what about him? Or the new young mom in town, disliking this move and too shy to find new friends—is there a place for her on your lunch schedule? The most common actions, when focused on the needs of others, become moments in which we serve the One who first served us.

When we dare to enter into the joys and sorrows of someone's life, something important takes place. A deeper, more profound joy arises in us that a pristine, well-kept busyness can never produce. As we gain an attentiveness to the presence of the Savior in the person we are serving, we experience a new intimacy in our relationship with Jesus. The nature of servanthood is that we give our full selves. In that kind of giving we come as close to the Savior as Simon did the day he trudged up a hill, carrying Jesus' cross.

That unexpected trip must have made a difference for Simon. God had something planned for him that day. Mark mentions Simon's two sons, Rufus and Alexander, as if they were well-known to the community for which Mark was writing. Ancient traditions even suggest that the two brothers accompanied Peter and Andrew on some of their missionary journeys. It seems that Simon and his family must have come to faith in Christ—the kind of dynamic faith that changed their lives and gave them fresh meaning and new direction—all because Simon took a moment out of his busy day to help a stranger along his sad and painful journey.

The peculiar math that Jesus uses is one of addition, not subtraction. We may be tempted to see servanthood as an interruption that subtracts something from life, but in Jesus' math, his heart for us, added to our time and resources for others, equals more than we started with. Our lives are enhanced by the proximity of Jesus in the people we serve. And that, in turn, equals joy.

Some Things to Think About

1. Think back over the past few days. What things "interrupted" your plans? Can you see any ways in which these interruptions might have been calls to serve?

2. How has daily living bent your attention inward? In what areas has your life seemed to have lost its focus?

3. What are your needs at this time? Bring them to Jesus in a prayer of petition. How do you need to be ministered to?

4. How does knowing that Jesus first served you make a difference in how you view serving someone who is difficult to serve? How does Jesus' serving you increase your joy in serving others?

5. Think of one person you may have been avoiding. What might you do to serve them?

6. For the next twenty-four hours, practice a heightened awareness. Take extra care to notice the opportunities for caring that come your way. Let yourself be open to interruptions as divine appointments.

chapter fourteen

What about Terri?

After this the Lord appointed seventy-two others
and sent them two by two ahead of him to every
town and place where he was about to go. He
told them, "The harvest is plentiful, but the workers are few. Ask the Lord of the harvest, therefore,
to send out workers into his harvest field."
(Luke 10:1-2)

I don't recall my life flashing before my eyes, but I
remember the panic surrounding me like the cold water,
draining my resolve as swiftly as the river current was
sapping my strength. In the end, I don't know if I would
have drowned. My only certainty is that when I needed
saving, a friend was there to rescue me.

My friends and I spent many summer days swimming in the Mississippi River, just north of Minneapolis.
An old tree stump jutted out from the high river bank,
with a rope tied to its branches, allowing us to swing out
over the river and drop into the water below. Normally,
we would swim back to shore and climb the cliff so we
could repeat the process. This time, however, we decided
that after diving into the water, we would swim to an
island in the middle of the river.

I was not a particularly strong swimmer, but neither
was I the type to be willingly left behind. I knew the

distance was a little more than I should attempt, but I decided to go for it anyway. Halfway across, I began to flounder, my head dipping beneath the water. Limbs that were supposed to push me through the current felt like lead fishing weights, dragging me to the bottom.

Finally, convinced my own strength was insufficient, I called out to my friends for help. I'd like to say they rushed directly to my aid. They didn't . . . because they didn't believe me! It wasn't a lack of concern that kept them swimming on without me. My friends simply misinterpreted my cry for help, believing it wasn't serious. They figured I was all right and could make it on my own. Not until they recognized the desperation in my voice did they take my situation as urgently as it demanded. Wrapping their arms around me, they pulled me to safety.

Once my friends moved into lifesaving mode, they did not waste time worrying if I would be offended at their rescue attempt, or, for that matter, whether I truly needed rescuing. They did not debate the impact their efforts would have on their own plans and pleasure. Nor did they look around for a professional lifesaver, one with all the training and expertise. If I were to be saved, it had to happen then and there, and they would have to take the responsibility. The need was real, and our relationship compelled them to take action.

Does all this seem obvious? I wonder. It occurs to me that there are countless numbers of people drowning in our world. We're surrounded by friends, neighbors, co-workers—even family—desperately paddling through life but sinking nonetheless. How do I know? I see them every day. So do you. And the saddest part? Many are left to drown alone when all around them are people who could save their lives.

I think of the first time I met Terri following a Christmas Eve service our congregation held in a local barn. A variety of people attended that service, some in jeans and others in fur coats. Sitting on hay bales instead of pews, shivering in the December night air, we reflected on how odd it was to be in a barn together on Christmas Eve—as odd for us as it was for the Son of God. Terri was present that night, hidden among the shadows at the back of the barn, not so much worshipping as wishing she could find for herself the peace she saw in others.

Terri later told me that she had come that night because a barn seemed less "churchy," a more neutral place for someone like her who had not been to a worship service in years. Terri began to tell me her story. Her uncle was "too friendly" as she was growing up. She was raped soon after high school and had born a child out of that moment of madness. She had married an alcoholic, who had given her more children before leaving her to fend for herself. Terri wanted to know why, though she had grown up attending church youth groups, God had vanished from her life.

"I can't seem to make a connection to God," she said. "It feels like I'm all on my own. There's this vacuum in my life that sucks everything in. It's a dark place where the only certainty is fear."

Terri's words haunted me like the murky images lingering in the dark following a nightmare. They woke me up from the easy slumber of a safe and comfortable faith, making it difficult for me to doze once again. Sometimes when I gather with my faith family for worship, as I find the comfort that supports me and the hope that strengthens me, I wonder . . . what about Terri?

Terri's not alone. I think of Kim, a high school girl who had become a friend of students in our youth group. Her parents didn't attend church, employing the well-worn cliché that they wanted their children to make their own choices about what faith—if any—they would hold. They didn't want to influence Kim's decision, they said, so they raised her with no faith at all. They did not send her to Sunday school; they would not bring her to worship. All in the name of freedom.

Kim explained that no one had ever told her about Jesus or encouraged her to meet him. No one had ever invited her to attend church with them; everyone wanted it to be her decision. Even those she knew best, friends who cared for her and on whom she relied the most, failed to share with her their relationship with Jesus, providing nothing of value from which she could choose. She never had a real choice because she had never been given a basis for choosing. When Sunday upon Sunday, I hear congregations of faithful Christians diligently pray for the spread of Christ's gospel to all people and places, I wonder . . . what about Kim?

The world is teeming with Kims and Terris. Chances are you know them; they are your neighbors, your friends, a family member. Maybe someone at school or on the job. They are people who have somehow missed out on experiencing firsthand the love of God in their lives. Perhaps somewhere, sometime, a negative episode in the church warped their view of faith. It could be they are confused, thinking that religion is little more than an unpalatable list of do's and don'ts designed to make them toe the moral line, with God as a cosmic cop waiting for them to slip so he can write up their infractions. Or perhaps everyone around them has misunderstood the seriousness of the situation, simply assuming they're not really drowning; they can swim just fine on their own.

Can you hear the desperate cries of the drowning? Listen carefully; they sound less like "help" and more like the frustration of people searching for something they can't quite place their fingers on. They are the voices of those looking for answers to questions that never quite seem to go away. They are the sounds of struggle over life issues that are never resolved. They are the cries of those whose strength is fading as they wait for someone to wrap them in the arms of a faith that can give them life.

If we believe the message we claim, then we must recognize that a world, a community, a family, an individual—anyone—trying to live apart from God is, in effect, drowning. Jesus' intention is that we would participate in a quite literal lifesaving operation.

In Luke 10, Jesus sent out seventy-two people with the assignment to go ahead of him and speak his message. These were not the twelve apostles, the first string, the experts. These seventy-two hadn't spent the time at Jesus' feet that Peter and John and James had; they weren't present for the transfiguration; they weren't in the boat when Jesus calmed the storm. They were people with jobs and families, commitments and a host of responsibilities. These were the rank-and-file followers, local folks, the ordinary faithful—simple servants like you and me.

Not long ago I reached the stage of life when it was college application time around our house. My kids were filling out the forms, taking SATs, ordering school transcripts, getting recommendations from teachers, and, of course, writing the obligatory essays. One recent application required something called a "proof of talent." Only after applicants demonstrated their worth, showed their value, proved their talent would the school deliberate and decide whether they would be invited to join.

Compare this to Jesus' application process: There wasn't any. Apparently, Jesus was a lot less discriminating. Jesus chose these seventy-two people without a single question. No tests needed, no references required, no proof-of-talent essays to prepare—not even an inquiry as to whether they might be interested in going. Just an invitation to hit the road. There was work to be done and lives to be saved. The only entrance requirement was their willingness to go in his name. Their task was the same as the apostles': heal the sick and proclaim the kingdom to anyone who would listen.

In preparing them for their ministry, Jesus reminded the seventy-two that not everything had to be perfect before they could go. He also knew that they would run into difficulties, that they risked rejection. None of that, however, was reason for hesitation. He sent them with confidence, and their strength came from him. And what was the outcome for these novices taking on this risky venture? When the seventy-two returned, Luke tells us they did so with joy.

Joy, like spring wildflowers, pops up throughout this story. Luke can't seem to hold it back. The seventy-two are joyful upon the completion of their mission. Jesus tells them to rejoice because their names are written in heaven. Even Jesus, Luke points out, rejoices upon hearing their good reports, the only time in the Gospel that Jesus' emotions are described in that way. I believe their joy came from the fact that, in all their ordinariness, they realized that by Jesus' command and commission, they had his power to help people, to rescue those who were drowning, to have a significant, eternal impact on the lives of people around them. And to think that Jesus rejoiced when he heard their good news . . . I can't think of a more profound reason for joy in life than that our simple act of faith sharing brings a smile to God's face.

Do you know what qualifies you as an evangelist? The same thing that qualified the seventy-two. Not a degree. Not a course in professional lifesaving. Not a careful theology. Just love.

It was love that compelled Christ to rescue us. He plunged into the hurt and sin and reached out a nail-scarred hand, pulling us from certain death and wrapping us in his mercy. As people who have been rescued, perhaps we understand more fully the urgency of reaching out to rescue others.

By the same token, it is love that compels us to share with others what we have. Love leaves no room for suggesting that the saving relationship Christ offered us has no merit for someone else. We cannot, in love, simply hope that people come equipped with some kind of built-in faith detector with which they will come to know the Lord without our ever having to speak a word. Love does not allow us to stand by, for fear that our rescue attempts will be perceived as offensive, while others sink. Jesus calls us to love people at the point of their greatest need, which is to know how "wide and long and high and deep is the love of Christ" (Ephesians 3:18). We do not have to put people in a headlock, but we can extend our arms.

It had been a long day, and at 10 P.M. we were just sitting down for dinner. The waitress serving our group of travelers and tourists in a little upstairs room a couple of blocks from our hotel in Beijing charmed us with her smile. She hovered near our table while the person in our group who spoke Chinese began a conversation with her. Her Chinese name translated as "Snowflake."

It turned out that Snowflake had moved to Beijing from nearly a thousand miles away, in the hopes of earning money and improving her English. She must have made very little—our group of sixteen ate a full dinner including Peking Duck and drinks for about thirty-five dollars—but she sent a portion of what she earned back to her family each month.

When we invited her to go with us the next day to see the Great Wall, she was eager to join us if she could get the day off. It was an unusual situation; we had expected her to say no. We were strangers to her, and quite a collection of strangers at that: a female African American pastor; Ron, who towered over six-and-a-half feet; Aina, a ninety-two-year-old woman; a Finnish pastor; a young woman and her mother; and three women who called themselves the wild widows.

But in the morning, there she was, in front of our hotel, ready to go.

It is common in China for people to adopt western names, and Snowflake asked us what hers might be. We chose the name Grace and explained to her what it meant. From that moment on she referred to herself as Grace, and a number of our group shared their faith with her and spoke to her of Jesus and his love.

At the end of the day, I asked Grace why she had come with us. She said that she had seen something special in our group and wanted to know more about it. She had found something that drew us all together, something she didn't see other places, and she liked it and wanted it.

On our last night in China, with tears filling her eyes and a catch in her voice, one of our group shared something that was in all our hearts: "I know now," she said, "why we are here together, and why we came to China. It was all for Grace."

You don't have to go to China to speak of Jesus' love. You can go next door. You can go to the next office over. The most significant evangelism happens within close relationships, with people whom we have meaningful connections. That's why Jesus told those he was sending to enter and live in a single house, so they might build relationships with people. By walking with others through their normal lives, we earn the trust and respect to be heard. Having gained that, we can speak of our love of Jesus.

And there is a sweet freedom to it all. When we have accepted Jesus' commission to go ahead of him into our towns, our neighborhoods, our circle of acquaintances, we can cease debating whether people really need rescuing. We can stop our continual soul-searching about whether we are suitable for, or comfortable with, the task. When we dive in, Jesus reminds us, as he did the seventy-two, that joy resides in the fact that our names are known in heaven. So is Terri's, Kim's, and Grace's. Their names are known, but will they know the One who knows their names? Perhaps. If someone introduces them.

Some Things to Think About

1. Think of a time when someone reached out to "rescue" you. What did they do for you? How did you feel about it?

2. If you were to chart your willingness to be Jesus' messenger, where would you put yourself on a scale from 1 to 10, with 10 being the position of dropping everything to go? What do you think holds you back? What are the inner arguments you have with yourself about speaking of Jesus' love?

3. In what way does it help to know that, when Jesus sent out the seventy-two, it had nothing to do with their qualifications or giftedness for evangelism?

4. How do you feel about Jesus rejoicing over your faith sharing? How do you feel knowing that Jesus has given you his power to help and rescue others?

5. In what way does knowing you have had a significant positive impact on others bring joy to your life?

6. Why is love the central ingredient in evangelism? Do you know someone like Terri or Kim? What might you do this week to reach out to them in love?

chapter fifteen

Keeping the Balance in Your Balancing Act

"Martha, Martha," the Lord answered, "you are worried and upset about many things, but only one thing is needed. Mary has chosen what is better, and it will not be taken from her."
(Luke 10:41-42)

The most remarkable thing about Chris was that she rode a bicycle with her father.

Chris was a freshman in my youth group, one of the more popular kids in her class. Her classmates regularly gathered around her, wanting to be her friend. Their conversations together were always animated affairs, their hands continually slicing the air. Chris was no teen fashion model; she would never be a cheerleader; no athletic team featured her as its star player. Still, Chris commanded the respect of everyone who knew her, young and old alike. For what was truly amazing about Chris was the way she walked, and how she rode that bicycle.

Chris was deaf. She had contracted meningitis when she was an infant, and it had completely destroyed her hearing. But communication was not her biggest challenge. Because the disease had ravaged her inner ear, Chris had very little innate sense of balance. Unlike most people who think nothing of walking, running, or cycling, Chris had to concentrate on her balance at all times. Walking required her to choose carefully where to place each foot, intentionally shifting her weight with each step in order to keep from toppling over. Still, Chris walked everywhere. And most inspiring to me? Chris could be seen regularly on summer evenings riding a tandem bicycle around the lake, sitting behind her dad as he balanced the bike for both of them.

Chris taught me two important things about balance: It's a crucial thing to have (though sometimes you don't realize that until it's gone); and when you lose it, you need to rely on someone who can restore it.

Life gets so easily out of balance, weighed down under mountains of responsibilities, distractions, and everyday tasks. It reminds me of my recent inbox: 401 messages. That's a lot of spam. When I left for vacation, I stopped checking my e-mail. 401 pieces of junk. 401 e-mails I did not want. 401 items I had to take the time to check and throw into the trash, all because someone else was certain I needed to know how to lower my mortgage rate (it's low enough, thanks), or buy cheap mail order drugs (I'm content with the drugs I already take), or make my partner happy (you can guess for yourself what those were about).

"Help," I whined to Jeff, our family tech-boy, "my computer is gorging itself on tasteless e-mails like I do on bacon at a breakfast buffet." That helped him understand the severity of the problem. He explained that I had to set my filters to screen out all that nonsense. With a few key strokes he turned my computer into a cyber version of the Patriot Act, examining each suspicious e-mail as it comes in, tagging the offenders as enemy combatants, and sending them, no questions asked, to the e-mail detention center. I don't think I'm winning the war; they're still out there looking for a way into my machine, but at least for the last few days I've received no—count 'em . . . zero, nada—spams. I love it.

Maybe your life seems a little like my inbox. People require your attention. One phone call isn't enough;

another beeps in, while a fistful more wait to be returned. Bills collect that should have been paid last week if you could just find the time to sit down and take care of them. But if you do, when will you carve out a moment to get to the post office for stamps?

People encircle you with requests. A hypnotic hum of activities commands your time and attention. It's October and they're still looking for a Sunday school teacher. How about you? Problems seem to multiply; complaints leave you feeling guilty.

Voices, voices—always asking, always wanting, always demanding. Advertisers pleading, shouting, enticing. Messages beamed at you about how you ought to look, what you ought to own, promising this and guaranteeing that. Crushing schedules. Interrupted plans. Impossible frustrations. Bedlam. Confusion.

The world charges at us like a crazed football player, ready to tackle. It's easy to lose our balance. Soon, we're believing that all this activity means something, that this is what life is all about. Soon, distractions become the focus. What was crucial slips to casual. The imperative turns immaterial.

In an unexpected twist, even the joy of servanthood can push us out of balance. That's what happened to Martha. Jesus and his disciples, on their way to Jerusalem, stopped by Mary's and Martha's home. The sisters welcomed them, and Martha set about providing the hospitality the Law of Moses required.

It didn't take long before a problem developed. It wasn't the amount of work that needed to be done. Nor was the real issue, despite Martha's complaints, the lack of help from Mary. Jesus identified the problem and came straight to the point. "Martha, you are worried and distracted by many things." Martha's heart was out of balance. She had lost her center.

Look at the shift: At first Jesus had been the center of Martha's efforts. But now she was irritated because Mary wasn't offering any assistance. In fact, Mary hadn't even noticed Martha's hard work! Martha suddenly felt taken for granted. Her attention had become focused not on what she was doing for the Lord, but on what Mary was not doing for *her*. That put Martha's actions and attitude out of harmony. Eternal Love was sitting right there in Martha's living room, and she had lost sight of him completely.

We, too, get out of balance when we feel over-committed and under-appreciated. When serving the needs of others seems more like an obligation than an opportunity, we have lost our center. When resentment swallows our ministry, when weariness drains our joy, chances are something is out of kilter.

Take note of Jesus' response: He didn't require Martha to do something else. Nor did he ask her to back off and give herself a break. He didn't tell her she shouldn't be engaged in what she was doing—after all, the work had to be done. We misunderstand if we think Jesus was telling Martha that she ought to be more like Mary, trading in her activity for a spot next to Mary. Martha's penchant for *doing* was not the issue. No, Jesus invited Martha to examine how the work itself had pushed her heart out of balance. Jesus simply wanted to get Martha's attention so she could re-focus on what was important. He wanted to break through all the distractions so he could restore her flagging spirit, and she could once again respond to his presence in her life.

Jesus' advice for Martha is the same for us when our lives are overloaded and our heart is out of balance: "Only one thing is needed. Choose what is better." In this marvelous economy of words, Jesus is telling us to center our lives once again on him. Turn to him and let him restore our balance.

Jesus' advice was born out of his own experience. Over and over throughout the Gospels, especially in Luke, we are told that Jesus went off to a lonely place to pray. That's an important statement not only for what it says but for what it *doesn't* say. We're not told that Jesus went off to a lonely place to take a vacation or soak in a hot tub. Nor did he lose himself in a distracting diversion or go to the beach to soak up a few rays. Those may be fine stress busters, but Jesus went off to a lonely place to *pray*. Sandwiched between the crushing demands of the people around him and the towns he was preparing to visit with his message, Jesus chose to spend time alone with God. It probably meant there were times when he was up late, or days when he arose early. But his time in prayer was too important to miss.

That's a good prescription to follow. Time alone with God can quiet the chaos. It can put things back into perspective and restore our balance by re-orienting us to the presence of God.

Fourteen hours is a long way to drive to get home. It's even longer when some of the time is spent driving at sixty-five miles per hour down the wrong road. One summer when we lived in Massachusetts, I took my family to visit Barbie's sister in Detroit. The quickest way there and back involved cutting across a portion of Canada. On the return trip, with everyone safely deposited in Michigan, I was preparing to cross back into the United States. Everything was zipping by and I wasn't paying a great deal of attention when I began to realize that things weren't looking familiar anymore. Exit signs bore labels for highways I didn't recognize. Mileage markers listed distances to places I wasn't going. I was moving fast, all right, but with no idea where I was headed or how to get back to where I wanted to be. The less sure I was of my route, the more irritated, frustrated, and angry I became. The less certain I was of whether this road would come out at the correct interchange, the more lost I felt and the more confused I became.

I finally realized that I had no choice. I had to get back on the right path—meaning I had to return to the beginning, to the spot where I had gone wrong in order to reorient myself and put my surroundings back in perspective. That's what Jesus meant when he told Martha, "Choose what is better."

Sooner or later, when serving others has worn us down or we stand amid the carnage of a busy life, we need to hear these words anew. We need to pause and let Jesus remind us where we find the meaning of life. We need to re-orient ourselves by spending time with him. Choosing what is better reshuffles our priorities so we can identify again what is important and allow what is less essential to become less urgent. When we re-center our lives on Jesus, we can find once again the fresh joy God intended.

It's been many years now since I watched Chris and her dad wheel that bicycle around. But what was true for them then remains true for us today. If you're uncertain about how to keep the balance in your balancing act, take a cue from a teenage girl circling a lake in the cool of the evening. Balance comes from your Father's hand.

Some Things to Think About

1. What things seem to throw your life out of balance?

2. Think of a time when you volunteered to do something that later became a burden, that built up resentment in you, that became more of an obligation than an opportunity. What was your original intent? To what did your focus shift?

3. How much time alone with God have you had in the past week? What got in the way of that time?

4. What are some of the "essentials" in your life that seem to have taken over?

5. Can you think of some times when you did something "for God" that interfered with *loving* God?

6. The most common answer to de-stressing life is to do less. How is that different from de-stressing through prayer? Think of some ways you can prioritize time with God.

chapter sixteen

The Value
of Clay Jars

But we have this treasure in jars of clay to show
that this all-surpassing power is from God and not
from us. (2 Corinthians 4:7)

The harsh squawk of the telephone cut through the
beginning of a Friday evening set aside for Campeau
family night. If this was dinner time, it had to be a
sales call. I got up from the table and stalked toward
the intruder, preparing to be polite but firm to the sales
person I was certain awaited me on the other end of
the line.

"Hello." I gave myself strict instructions: Don't let
them ask me how I am; beat them to the punch; say no
thanks before they get started on a sales pitch.

"Reverend Campeau?" The tone in the caller's voice
made it immediately clear this was no sales call. "This
is Judy from the Emergency Room at Jordan Hospital.
There's been an accident. One of your members. I think
you need to get down here right away."

"I'll be right there." A quick explanation to Barbie
and the kids, and I was out the door.

What had happened? It sounded serious, but how serious? A leaden September sky crouched close to the earth with the remnants of an early autumn rain. I reached for the local radio station. A report was just coming in. Names I recognized.

Some kind of car collision. Few details.

It is my practice to pray before entering a hospital. Prior to sharing some words with those I am visiting, I share some words with God. That night I prayed them more intensely than ever before.

"Lord, I'm not sure what is about to happen. I don't know what I will say. Please, don't let my inabilities stand in the way of the ministry of your Spirit. Let me be open and attentive to what you would say and do through me."

When I arrived at the emergency room, Judy, the nurse who had called, met me at the desk and led me to the waiting area. Two youth from my congregation—sisters—had been driving home from soccer practice. The tires had lost traction on the damp street, and the car had struck a tree. One girl was hurt but would recover. Chrissy, fourteen years old, had not survived.

"Mom is in here," Judy explained as we paused in the hallway. "The doctor will be in soon to explain things. Dad is on his way home from a business trip, and we have been unable to contact him."

Judy opened the door, and I stepped in to see Silvia sitting on the other side of the room. I embraced her, saying nothing. She knew, she said, that Chrissy was dead. Her concern was for her older daughter who, though she was not responsible, would feel that heavy burden nonetheless. And her husband, who would notify him? And her other two younger children, who would stay with them? I arranged for my wife, Barbie, to go to the house so Silvia could remain at the hospital and wait for Bill.

I spent the rest of the evening at the hospital. We went together to another part of the emergency room to check on Chrissy's sister who wanted to know the unbearable news she had already guessed. I stood by as Bill arrived, and he and Silvia cried the anguished tears that no parent should ever have to shed. I waited for them, and prayed, as they went in to say their good-byes to their daughter. In the days ahead there would be a funeral, and then follow-up calls with this family for whom crushing tragedy had ground all joy to dust.

In the weeks that followed, I wondered: Had I served this family when they needed me? Eight years of training and ten years of experience had not adequately prepared me for those hours at the hospital.

Was there something I should have said? Was there more I could have done? It seemed as if I had spent the entire night floundering for words that would offer more than empty puffs of air. I fumbled, afraid that any comfort I might offer would sound too easy, my words of hope too hollow. The prayers I prayed felt weak and limp. So I said very little that night. I just held their hands and put my arms around their shoulders, trying to know when to come close and when to allow some distance and privacy.

I felt so helpless, so inept. What on earth was I doing? Who deemed me able, worthy of carrying such a responsibility as ministering to people overwhelmed by undeserved pain? How could my meager skills fill the gaping needs of this family with whom I shared the hurt? What made me think that anything I did could soothe the ragged wound in their lives?

Times of sitting with people who are sick, or suffering through pain and tragedy, are not reserved for the clergy. Sooner or later we all find ourselves in situations where our comfort and ministry is needed. Perhaps it is a family member. Maybe a friend. And what then?

Those are the moments when we don't have answers. Words do not come, and all we have to offer are tears or a silent embrace. Insecurities about our ability to handle the situation ridicule our attempts to minister to those whose need overpowers our skills. We feel as if we've let them down. Maybe we've even let God down. And we wonder: How can God accomplish anything through such inept servants?

Then again, God seems to delight in working through the most unlikely characters. If you're not sure, take a few minutes and scan the names listed in Matthew 1:1-16. It's a genealogy. A family tree. Jesus' family tree, to be precise. This passage doesn't often get much attention. Not much devotional material here. These verses aren't very conducive to group discussion. Might as well move past them to the good stuff in the story of Jesus' birth. If you do, however, you'll miss something important.

This list of Jesus' forebears is far from a stellar cast of admirable people. Rahab? She was a prostitute. David? Granted, he was a king, but he was also an adulterer. Ever heard of Ram? Probably not. Ram is one of the faceless people of the Bible, too ordinary to stand out. The only thing known about him is that he was the son of Hezron and the father of Amminadab. Odd that God would use folks like these to bring about the birth of Jesus. And yet in each case, God took common people in ordinary situations and accomplished extraordinary things.

Is it any stranger, then, that God would choose to use you? Call God crazy, if you will. Accuse God of bad taste or being a poor judge of character. Maybe you think God has a knack for picking the talentless folks. Defying human logic, God steadfastly insists on pouring out the Spirit in all the wrong places to accomplish all the right things.

Paul explains it like this in 2 Corinthians 4:5-12: When we have something valuable, we put it in a secure place. We lock it away in a safety deposit box, hide it in a secret spot, take out an insurance policy to protect it. But God operates differently. God takes risks. Instead of placing the treasure of the Spirit in a safe place, protected and unreachable, God places it in the most visible, vulnerable spot of all. Like storing the Hope Diamond in a humble clay jar, God places the Spirit in us!

By placing this treasure in so public a place as your life, and mine, God writes us into a great adventure that touches and heals and gives hope to the people—as ordinary as ourselves—who walk in and out of our lives. God's treasure in us means nothing less than God is invested in our lives.

Nothing spectacular about you, you say? Nothing God can use? Your talent is small, your gifts are the discount variety from the markdown table? The issue, says Paul, is not the quality of the container but the value of the treasure it carries. What's important is not the warmth of your personality or the strength of your faith. What's key are not the abilities you think you have or the talents you're afraid you lack. What's crucial are not the answers you've figured out or the words you choose to say. At stake is the grace and power of God who works through you, and yes, despite you. All God requires for this arrangement to succeed is your willingness to turn to the One who can do what you cannot.

When I was a pastor in Massachusetts, our congregation made the decision to purchase and renovate the house next to our church building. We were in desperate need of Sunday school and office space, and when the house went on the market, we saw the solution to our problem. The first major task was to move some of the interior walls to make the building more functional for our purposes. That's when I discovered the principle of load-bearing walls. Some walls in the house supported the entire structure and could not be moved.

With plaster covering the framing, and wallpaper on top of that, these particular walls didn't stand out; on the surface they looked like every other wall. It was their hidden beams, each a certain thickness and placed at strategic locations, that bore the weight of the entire building. Nothing could stand without them. All our plans had to take them into account.

When the project was finally complete—new walls in place, fresh carpet on the floor, bright new lights shining on carefully painted walls—the building barely resembled its former self. But still in place, hidden from view, those load-bearing timbers continued to do their work, holding everything together and keeping the house standing. In the end, paint and wallpaper are nice, but it's the beams beneath the surface that do the work.

And it is God, whose Spirit is sometimes nearly imperceptible within us, who does the ministering. In one of God's ironic twists, even the inadequacy and powerlessness we feel so fully, and against which we struggle so mightily, are gifts. When we stop trying to compensate for our weaknesses, we are driven to a reliance on the God whose treasure is the grace and strength that lies within us. We turn to a God who can be for others all that we cannot.

That's how weakness becomes strength. At the very moment when we walk into a situation we can't handle ourselves, for which we have no answers and none of our words sound right, that is when we need to breathe the words, "You handle it through me, my friend, because I can't." It is at that precise moment that God is most powerfully at work. The situation that seems to exhaust us, leaving us broken and confused, becomes the place where God exists most powerfully and God's love becomes most real. When we let God do what we cannot, God can do extraordinary things.

Our job is not to bear the weight of the house; that's for God to do. Nor are we the ones called to heal the pain of others; the Lord will take care of that. But that doesn't mean we should draw back from comforting the hurting; that's why God calls us together. That doesn't mean we should be afraid of helping the helpless; that's the mission God has given us.

What is important is knowing that when we are unsure, despite our inability or fear, God's power is at work to make a difference in people's lives through us. We may be just jars of clay, but we each carry within us a treasure. When we keep the relationship between the container and the treasure it carries in focus, we will be free to serve in confidence and joy.

A standing joke around our house is the difference between the way Barbie opens gifts and the way I do. She carefully lifts each individual piece of tape off the package, gently unfolds the wrapping where it has been creased, meticulously refolds the paper again into a neat square, and only then moves on to see what the gift is. I am a ripper. As far as I am concerned the whole point of wrapping paper is to tear through it to get to the gift it contains. When it is Barbie's birthday, gift opening can take the better part of the evening; when it is my birthday, it is startling how quickly the wrapping lies in shreds on the floor. For me it is all about the gift, not the wrapping.

The significance of our days lies in the fact that they are the wrapping paper for the gift of God's presence in the world. Our God is not a mediocre God, a passable God of middling talent who is content just to get by. Ours is a God of excellence and wonder, of majesty and a deep joy that pulses through creation. God holds nothing back, but fills us with the tremendous gift of the Spirit. There is no more compelling invitation in life than to serve that excellent God. And in doing so, our joy comes not from our own estimation of our skills, but from the gift we carry within. Our confidence is grounded not in our abilities but in the One who has poured into these clay jars all the value, all the priceless treasure, we will ever need.

Some Things to Think About

1. Think of a time of crisis when you felt helpless and didn't know what to say or do. How did you pray then?

2. On a scale from 1 to 10, with 10 being the highest, where would you place your value to your family? To your work? To your church? To God?

3. What weight(s) are you trying to "hold up" in your life right now? What pressures do you feel to fix something or take care of someone?

4. How do you think your desire to be strong can interfere with God's desire to work in you? What do you need to hand over to God's care?

5. Think of a time when you experienced God working through you, even though you didn't feel adequate.

6. Pray a prayer of thanksgiving for the gift of God in you.

chapter seventeen

The Joy
of a Generous Heart

Calling his disciples to him, Jesus said, "I tell you the truth, this poor widow has put more into the treasury than all the others. They all gave out of their wealth; but she, out of her poverty, put in everything—all she had to live on."
(Mark 12:43-44)

We are created to give; it is in our nature. Stronger than simply adhering to a moral code, the need to give courses through us as a defining characteristic of who we are. If you need evidence, spend some time watching toddlers.

I know what you're thinking: Toddlers are selfish! They learn very quickly how to stake their claims with a piercing "Mine!" It is no coincidence that at precisely the same moment they also begin to wail over the things they want and do not have. It is a grieving that will last, perhaps, for the rest of their lives. But before that stage— at a still younger age—before they realize the power and pain of possessions, toddlers know innately how to give.

The two little ones for whom Barbie cares play a game common to every toddler who has ever waddled across a room. The game begins as I sit down on the couch. Within moments, they come to me, each carrying a gift: a toy, a book, a partially chewed cracker. The gift itself is unimportant. It's the giving they're interested in. They hold out the offering, waiting for me to take it. But here is where an understanding of the game is key. If I take the gift, say thank you, and keep it, I have violated an important rule and will be met with a quizzical look or perhaps tears. No, when I receive the gift, there is only one thing to do, and it's obvious to any toddler: say thank you and give it back. That's what allows the fun to continue, for then the child can give it to me once again, and the game goes on. The only response that short-circuits the fun is when I'm so foolish as to keep the gift without giving it away.

One day, when Jesus was sitting in the temple, he spotted a lonely widow who understood that paradox of giving.

Jesus must have liked to observe people. I think he would be comfortable in a modern airport or the center court of a local mall, watching people as they pass. The stories he used in his teaching, the examples that found their way into his speech, regularly had about them the familiarity of the ordinary—seeing in common life illustrations of the eternal.

This particular day was no different. Jesus rested against one of the temple pillars, his attention focused on the milling crowd of praying, talking, walking people. One by one, they wandered over to the temple treasury to make their deposits, thinking they were purchasing a little more favor from their accountant God, enjoying the conspicuous sound the heavy coins made as they fell into the box.

But over there, small and quiet and nearly lost among the crowd, Jesus noticed another person approaching the offering box. She wore the telltale clothes of the desperately poor. This was a person with such little financial stability that she barely had two thin, nearly worthless coins to rub together. Jesus watched her as she put them both in the offering.

Here was a woman who came with nothing but left with everything. She arrived in ragged poverty, her status as a widow a guarantee that she would always be one of society's forgotten; yet she left as the most fulfilled person in the crowd. Shuffling through the temple, she served as an easy mark for the pompous and arrogant who needed a painless standard by which they could compare themselves; yet she departed amid words of praise and the recognition of her Savior. She was a woman of absolutely no financial means; yet she gave a larger offering than the comfortably middle-class folks who haunted the sanctuary and congratulated themselves on their generosity.

That is the paradox of giving. Far from resulting in having less for ourselves, giving kindles a glowing joy. Instead of depleting our resources of money, time, or energy, giving can replenish our gladness. In giving, we experience a refreshing internal harmony, for we become more fully who we were meant to be. That was the joy at work in the woman Jesus observed, and it is a joy available to anyone in any circumstance if we understand the wisdom of the widow. It is the joy that comes from a generous heart. The only thing that short-circuits the joy God intends is when we receive God's gifts and forget to give them away.

Some of the most quietly jubilant people I meet are those who know how to give. They find it easy. For me, it's more of a challenge. While I am likely to clutch at a dollar bill, seeing in its loss a diminishing of my life, those who view life as an opportunity to give seem untroubled by the turmoil of gaining and maintaining. It's as if they have known all along that the only way to completely enjoy the Giver's gifts is to return them to the Giver by turning them loose in the service of those in need. While I may glance at the check register to calculate the impact of my giving, or check the daytimer to see if I can afford the time that caring will require, there are those who give first and check later. You know the people I'm describing: givers whose contentment with life seems nearly unshakable.

The book of Genesis spells out how we are created in God's image, how we are fashioned after God. Do you know anyone who can out-give God? The essence of God is a Giver. God placed Adam and Eve not in some broken-down heap of a creation, but in a lush, teeming garden. God befriended Abraham and offered to make him a great nation. God gave manna when his people were hungry, a home when his people were wandering, a Son when his people were hopeless. And on top of a hill on a spring afternoon, where a cross raked the darkening sky, God gave his most lavish gift, thereby ensuring that your life and mine will last forever. God gives; it is who God is. To be created in God's image means we are created to give as God gives, with passion and abandon, without reservation. It is who we are meant to be.

Many of us live our lives as if we were two people trapped within a single body. There is the person immersed in calculating costs, setting priorities, managing resources, and determining profits and losses. But existing within us is also the person we know God meant us to be, the person of God's creative passion, the person who was born to give. When we give with a generous heart, we allow the Spirit to sing into harmony the person we are with the person we were created to be, and that in turn restores wonder to our lives. When we share ourselves—a common embrace, a particular talent, a portion of our income, a measure of our time—we return the gift first given us, and we tap into a reservoir of joy.

Joyous people are givers, and givers are, at heart, lovers. Giving bubbles forth from a pool of love, for it is always a matter of the heart. The deepest impulses of our hearts—not a sense of duty or compulsion—give rise to the most profound and generous gifts we give. God does not need to pry a few coins from our locked fingers or a few minutes from our panicked schedules. God does not want to pry a little response from our protected hearts. God is not after our money. God is after us.

When the widow gave all she had, she gave all she was. In giving her penny, she was giving herself. Jesus made it clear: What was important was not the amount she gave, but what giving her last penny represented. While the rest of the people offered only what they could comfortably spare, her gift came from her heart and represented both tremendous sacrifice and unwavering love.

Sitting next to my computer for a number of years was a large cross. It stood about four feet high and was constructed from cast-off, splintered, partially painted old pieces of two-by-four lumber. The figure of Jesus was made from scrap pieces of cedar shingles and was fastened to the cross with bent nails. At the spot where Jesus' hands and feet should have been, red paint was dabbed onto the wood to represent his blood. His face was fashioned from the bottom of a plastic plate; eyes, nose, and mouth, and a crown of thorns, were colored on with crayon. A loin cloth consisted of a disposable diaper, and a message had been carved with a wood-burning set on another shingle above Jesus' head: "Here's the king of the Jews." This odd crucifix was an anniversary present from our children, who had labored together long and hard to produce it and surprise us. But in reality, the gift had nothing to do with the cross, for it was a gift of themselves, given not from obligation but from the heart because love compelled it. But then again, maybe it had everything to do with the cross.

At the source of any gift—money, time, or anything of value—lies love. If we don't give well, perhaps it is not the giving we find difficult but the loving it involves. If we give but count the cost, we give out of duty and not out of love. If we give only after determining that the giving will require no real sacrifice, we've not given, we've loaned. If we give with a self-important sigh, it's not our head that's hard, it's our heart. We pay bills because they must be; we settle debts to win freedom from obligation; only gifts carry love with them.

For the widow with her penny, giving was a matter of the heart. Her love for God could do nothing else but give itself without reservation. As our heart is, so will our giving be. And as our giving is, so will our joy be.

Some Things to Think About

1. Think of the last gift you gave (i.e., a birthday present, a thoughtful note, some volunteer time, a check to the church). How did you feel about giving this gift?

2. Jesus, in pointing to the widow, suggests that there are times when giving a lot is still giving only a little, while at other times giving only a little is in reality giving a great deal. Where do you find that principle at work in your life?

3. Make a list with two columns. Label the one on the left "My Generous Heart" and list some times/occasions when you have given freely, joyously. Label the one on the right "My Calculating Mind" and list some times/occasions when you have given out of duty, deciding what you could/should offer. Take a few moments to consider your lists. What do these occasions tell you about your giving?

4. Think of a time when someone gave you a gift and you knew they felt *wonderful* about being able to give it. How did you feel about receiving it?

5. What do you think are the connections between being a gracious gift receiver and a generous gift giver?

6. Think of someone for whom you would like to do something with a generous heart. Plan how you will do that in the coming week.

chapter eighteen

What's in It for Me?

"... whoever wants to become great among you must be your servant, and whoever wants to be first must be your slave—just as the Son of Man did not come to be served, but to serve, and to give his life as a ransom for many."
(Matthew 20:26-28)

I guess Jesus couldn't help himself. He was not one to pass up the opportunity to stand reasonable human expectations on their head. Look at how he handled the simple request of a protective mother.

She didn't come right out and say it, but she was looking at the bottom line for her sons. "Jesus, what do they get out of this?" It's a good question for a mother to ask when she's watching out for her children. It was a simple, understandable query coming from one who only wanted the best for her boys.

"Jesus," said the mother of John and James, "my sons have been following you for quite some time now. They do what you want and go where you go. They preach what you tell them and believe what you say. They've been with you almost from the beginning. They're good boys. You know you can depend on them. You don't suppose they could get a cabinet post in your administration, do you?"

When the rest of the disciples found out what the Zebedee boys' mom had been asking, they were a little put out. Before long, they were not just walking along in a sullen mood, they were grumbling loud enough for Jesus to hear. Were they shocked at the extent to which Jesus' message had been misunderstood? Not quite. Were they offended that someone should bother the Master with such trivial, self-centered concerns? Hardly. The disciples were upset because their friends' mother had had the nerve to ask for that which they wanted just as badly for themselves. She had beaten them to the punch, and that meant they might lose out on their share of the reward. One mother and twelve disciples, and they all had the same question: "Where's the payoff? What's in it for me?"

It's the same question humanity has been asking since the serpent convinced Eve that God was holding out on her. It turns out that we're not much different than the Zebedee boys' mom. We, too, want to know what the payoff for following Jesus is. Perhaps we're not as blatant in our inquiries, but we still want to know about the benefit package. The reward of faith, we think, ought to lift us out of the mire of everyday life. The benefits of belief ought to temper the difficulties of daily existence. I have a friend who likes to sum up much of the current evangelical message with the words of a familiar song sung with an adjusted emphasis: "Jesus loves ME, this I know."

What can you do for me, Jesus? Will you stabilize my marriage? Will following you make me successful? You will shield me from pain, won't you? Will my discipleship protect my kids? Will I get a leg up on personal finances because I tithe? Can I earn any bonus points in the peace and happiness category? Can you assure me that I will shiver with emotion each time I worship? I know you're offering a pledge of eternal life, but I'm just wondering what kind of short-term returns I might expect on my investment.

Perhaps, without even realizing it, we tie discipleship to a reward. We talk a good game when it comes to grace—

we even cringe when someone suggests that our salvation is a benefit of good behavior—but at the same time, we expect that following Jesus will somehow result in tangible blessings. We certainly don't expect our struggles to continue, let alone intensify, after we've met Jesus.

Somehow, in this self-absorbed generation, the focus of our faith has shifted from the promise of heaven to the desire for immediate rewards; from Jesus' invitation to serve and follow, to what following will do for us personally. Great nineteenth-century hymns looked forward to "the home I treasure." Not anymore. Now we're more intent on Jesus "filling our cup 'til it overflows." In our day, discipleship, like everything else, is subject to cost analysis and profit-and-loss statements.

Is it crass? Perhaps. Is it the way of the world? Absolutely. We are soaked in a popular culture that worships power, wealth, style, and recognition—and all the advantages these things provide. We're dazzled by the starlet, the tycoon, the princess.

A bizarre convergence of events took place in September, 1997, shedding a revealing light on what we deem important. The world witnessed two funerals in the same week. Both were for well-known people, but that was where the similarities ended.

The first funeral commanded a week's worth of around-the-clock media attention. Network anchors were on the spot, reporting every detail, analyzing every agonizing moment and then analyzing it again, finally serving it all up for a public so enthralled with the tragedy and its aftermath that they left ten thousand tons of flowers at a palace gate. Unwilling to miss a moment, they arose by the millions early on a Saturday morning to participate in the final good-bye. Princess Diana—not to minimize her charitable efforts—was not the subject of our fascination because of her good works. The celebrity-driven magazines fed us a steady diet of the twists and turns of her fairy-tale life gone sour, and updated us continuously on her latest look. We could not rip our attention away.

The other funeral that week was for a mother whose children were the unfortunate human refuse of a world that does not know what to do with its poor. While world dignitaries also attended Mother Teresa's funeral, it commanded comparatively little media attention. Few friends paraded before the public to dissect the intricacies of her life. No one suggested that her passing would somehow transform a nation or a world. We cried copious tears for Diana; we were briefly saddened by Mother Teresa's passing.

Ours is a world that covets the very things that Jesus most steadfastly refused to offer. Ours is a life so entrenched in the way the world works that we expect our discipleship to function the same way. That's why, though we comprehend Jesus' words about discipleship, we have a difficult time fitting them into the contours of our life. It's like trying to transplant a new heart while leaving the old one still beating in place.

Jesus' answer to the Zebedee mom's request included nothing of imminent rewards, special places of honor, or world-class perks. Here, as in other places, Jesus concentrated on a cup that had to be drunk, on a life that included risk and sacrifice, on a path that would lead inevitably to servanthood and a cross. As he often did, Jesus' words turned his disciples'—and our—expectations upside down, inside out, and backward: if you want to be great, be servants; if you want to be first, be last; if you want to live, be prepared to die; if you think following means crowns and thrones, be ready for thorns and a cross.

It's an answer we would rather not hear.

Some years ago, I took our youth group into central Los Angeles for a weekend of learning and serving through a local rescue mission. One of our young people had a prior commitment and needed to join our group late. She had made arrangements to have her mother bring her to the mission so she could meet up with us.

Outside the building, scores of people were gathered, camping out on the sidewalk and milling in front of the door, waiting to be admitted. I didn't want our student's mother to simply drop her off, so one other adult and I decided to go outside and wait for her. We sat on the curb, becoming a momentary part of the crowd, and we waited. We were scruffy from having stayed in one of the local flop house hotels for a couple of nights, and we probably blended in pretty well with the other street people gathered around make-shift fires there on the sidewalk. A car drove by, and another, and another after that as we sat there. After a while, I noticed a couple in one of the passing cars pointing a video camera out the window, recording the whole scene.

Suddenly I was going to be on someone's vacation video, looking exactly like the people I was there to help, a homeless man surrounded by life's casualties. I found myself in that miserable place wanting to throw my hands up and shout to the couple in the car, "Wait a minute! Don't take my picture. I don't really belong here. I live in the suburbs. I've got a job and a family and a home. I don't have the same weaknesses or illnesses or hard luck that had landed these people here. I'm not one of them; I'm just here to help." It was okay to help, but it was not okay to be one of them. And the truth is, I was not one of them, because at the end of the day I would return to my home, take a hot shower in my own bathroom, change into fresh clothes, eat dinner with my family, sleep in my own bed, and leave it all behind. It was their world, not my world, and I didn't really want to be a part of it; I just wanted to help out.

In that moment I realized I had never quite grasped the full impact of what Jesus' call to discipleship means. It has nothing to do with having our desires granted or our needs met. Discipleship is an opportunity to go where he goes and serve those he serves. It's not about trying to reconcile Jesus' words with our values; it's about changing our values so they reflect his.

When we measure the value of our service by how good it makes us feel or how much we get out of it, that smothers our joy. Placing ourselves at the center of what we do is likely in the end to leave us feeling disappointed. When we try to gauge what we do based on personal benefits, we end up exhausted from the effort of making sure that we're getting what we need and want. When we carefully avoid things that will leave us tired, we might miss the things that fulfill us the most. When we do something for praise and then don't get as much as we think we deserve, we end up feeling bitter. Continuously looking for ways for our service to fulfill our own needs is an endless game. We can run ourselves ragged trying to feel good about what we're doing so we can feel good about ourselves.

Jesus suggests a better way. Rather than asking, "What's in it for me," Jesus tells us to follow his example: to serve rather than be served.

These words from Jesus are not so much a command as a promise. When we drink from his cup, when we ingest into our lives those things that connect us to Jesus and his suffering, it may involve some pain. We may wind up putting our lives on the line for the sake of others. We will become sensitized to others' pain. We will discover our weaknesses.

But we also will find genuine joy, not as a dreamlike abstract, but as the well-worn reality of a servant's life. Just as sin is its own punishment and complacency its own prison, so is discipleship its own reward. For when we live in imitation of Jesus, we will find ourselves with one goal and one love, with a single vision and a single need: to know ourselves accepted by Christ and to live our lives for him. When we give ourselves to him and to all those he loves, when we give all of ourselves—not just that which is left over and easy to give—then we are in the company of Jesus, who gave himself for us. And that is more than enough.

The most telling part of the episode in Matthew 20 is the context in which it occurred. Jesus had just talked about what was awaiting him in Jerusalem. For the second time he had predicted his suffering and death. It was at that very moment that momma and the boys decided to start asking about how close their thrones would be to the Big One. In spite of what Jesus had just said, their first concern was what was in it for them.

But notice Jesus' reaction. Pay attention to his patience. He didn't explode at their dimness, or blow up at their blindness, or despair at their foolishness. He didn't do it to them, nor will he do it to you. His love won't waver in the face of your waffling. His mercy isn't diminished by the weight of your mistakes. His compassion doesn't collapse when confronted with your complaints. He simply, once again, invites you to follow along in joy in the adventure of his grace.

That's what's in it for you.

Some Things to Think About

1. What kinds of things make you grumble? Ponder for a moment about expectations you have that are not being met.

2. What things in your life seem to run you ragged, rob you of joy? What are some of the benefits you keep hoping to get from doing these things?

3. What are some of the joys of service that you have experienced?

4. How would you describe the connection between joy and following Jesus with no expectation of immediate reward?

5. What are you hoping Jesus will do for you? Take this time to tell him about your expectations.

6. Prayerfully consider a place where you might offer your service this week.

chapter nineteen

Loving Outside the Lines

. . . Jesus withdrew to the region of Tyre and Sidon. A Canaanite woman from the vicinity came to him, crying out, "Lord, Son of David, have mercy on me!" (Matthew 15: 21-22)

On a Friday afternoon in western Colorado, I discovered, much to my surprise, that I am one of *them*. Until that moment, I had been blissfully unaware of my status. My mother had never prepared me for being one of *them*, so I didn't know what to expect. I didn't even see it coming. But, like it or not, I had to face the harsh reality; I am . . . one of *them*.

We were heading home from a vacation that had taken us to Denver. It was lunch time, and while we had put a number of miles behind us, we still had too many more to go. Time to get out and stretch the legs at a rest stop just outside of Grand Junction. We broke out some sandwiches, and as the rest of the family arranged the picnic table, I decided to visit the information building. That's where I came face-to-face with the awful truth.

While looking over the rack of brochures, I couldn't

help but hear the conversation taking place just over my left shoulder.

"You getting many people from California?" asked an older woman.

I could feel my pride awaken. She was asking about my state. I confess: I like living in California.

"Many?" observed the other woman behind the information counter. "They're moving here by the carload. New ones coming every day. Pretty soon they'll take over."

I thought I could hear the hissing sound of my self-worth deflating like a punctured balloon.

"What do people around here think of it, all them Californians coming?" the first woman wanted to know.

"They're evil," said the information agent. "They move in and expect all the services they had in California. They want to change things so it's just like what they left. But no one here is all that interested in that, I'll tell you." And then, just for good measure, "Yep, I say they're evil."

I couldn't believe it. Wait a minute. Sure, we in California have had our share of problems: earthquakes, fire, floods, riots, embarrassing trials, to name a few. But *evil?* Suddenly I found myself lumped randomly together with all the other "evil Californians," not for who I was but because of a label someone had assigned to me.

I thought about protesting. "Hold on," I wanted to say. "You're talking about me. I'm nice. I don't want to change anything here. I'm a family man, a minister, for goodness sake. You've got nothing to fear from me."

I admit, it was a first-time experience for me. I'm white, born in this country; I'm middle class, heterosexual, and male. I've never been one of *them* before, and I didn't like it. It left me feeling hurt and angry. Belittled. I felt isolated and unimportant. These two women had drawn a boundary indicating who were acceptable people. They had drawn lines around those deemed welcome in their community, and it clearly did not include me. I was outside the lines.

Had they realized what was happening, they would most likely have offered an embarrassed retraction: "Oh, we didn't mean *you.*" But that's how it is when we draw lines. We never plan to exclude people. It's usually rather subtle, buried under good intentions, careless conversations, and unintended meaning contained in unexamined actions. Unconsciously, perhaps, we push and pull people into impersonal groups because we're more comfortable dealing with them that way.

Still, the truth remains: as soon as there is a *them,* it leaves no room for *us.* When as a community, a nation, or a church we divide ourselves, there is no longer a whole. Even if the lines we draw are unintentional, the result is still the same: Those who are not in are out. Someone is left beyond the circle.

We grow up drawing lines: who to play with and who to avoid. We learn to color inside the lines at the same time we learn to love in a similar manner. School life is a process of separating and being separated into categories based on grade point averages, athletic ability, and friendships.

With age, the lines become deeper and more significant. The color of our skin; the accent of our speech; the car we drive; the house we own; the job we hold; the bank account balance on which we draw; our nation of origin; our gender; the bent of our politics; whether we're on welfare or work—they all have the potential to put us on different sides of the line.

Our world and our lives are webbed with lines that divide and hide, lines that sap our love leaving us empty, isolated, and joyless. For if we love only inside the lines, we never learn to love as Jesus does, for he loves outside all boundaries.

Just ask the Caananite woman whose story Matthew tells in chapter 15. She was desperate. Her daughter was suffering, and like any mother, she was determined to find help from any source. Gathering her courage, this woman, who was clearly one of *them,* called out to a Man whom convention dictated she had no business bothering.

Understand the dynamics of the situation. As a Caananite, she was an outsider, a foreigner, someone held in contempt by the children of Abraham. But that wasn't all: She also was a woman. In her culture, she had no value as a person apart from the husband to whom she was married. She was as far outside the lines as one could get, and no self-respecting Judean man would have had anything to do with her.

Even Jesus' disciples were becoming impatient. This whole scene was unnecessary, as far as they were concerned. They were ready to dismiss her. "Send her away," they said. "You don't need to deal with her."

What follows is a difficult conversation to understand. Jesus sounded harsh, even rude. He didn't sound at all like the Jesus we expect. He told this woman that he was sent only for the house of Israel, which by implication did not include her. Still she persisted, kneeling and pleading before him. Again, Jesus appeared to rebuff her, saying that food for the children shouldn't be wasted on the dogs. What was going on?

Remember, however, that we have only the words. We cannot hear his tone of voice or see his facial expressions. Jesus had just come from an argument with the Pharisees, those men who spent their lives drawing lines of exclusion around others based on how carefully they followed the Pharisee's own interpretation of God's law. Perhaps the tone in Jesus' voice was satirical; maybe he was playing with the very reply others expected him to give the woman. Every Pharisee, disciple, and "in" person would have said, "She's one of them, a Caananite. Jesus really shouldn't do anything for her."

But then he does! Her faith is great and her daughter is healed. The real miracle here, more astounding than any healing, is that Jesus loved outside the lines.

That's the way it is with Jesus. Jesus loves outside the lines because he refuses to love groups and instead loves individuals. While we draw lines, make distinctions, pronounce judgment, Jesus' love cuts across boundaries, transcends differences, and offers mercy. For Jesus, no one stands outside the lines. No one.

That's the kind of love to which Jesus calls us. When it is present in our lives, joy accompanies it; when it is missing, we lose touch with the Savior into whose likeness we are being transformed. To love in Jesus' way begins with owning up to the lines we draw.

I could hear them just outside the office, and I knew immediately who they were. It was a Sunday afternoon, everyone at church had long since left, and as the pastor, I was the only one still around. Or at least I was the only one supposed to be there.

I confirmed my suspicions as I opened the door onto the expanse of our concrete patio. Three skateboarders. Kids. Young ones. They were twisting and turning, foul language spewing from their pre-adolescent mouths, doing their skateboarding thing directly under a large red sign that said "No Skateboarding!"

I was angry. Pointing to the sign, I asked, "What does that sign say?"

"No skateboarding."

"Does it refer to you?" I challenged.

"I guess so."

"Your skateboards mark up and damage the concrete, and then we have to clean it up and repair it. If you want to mark up someone's concrete, I suggest you mark up your own."

They left without another word.

Sliding into my car for the drive home, I realized I was still angry. At first I thought I was irritated with those three kids and their wretched skateboards. Didn't they have any regard for other people and their property?

Then I thought I was annoyed with their parents. Why does it seem so many baby boomers, of which I am one, insist upon being such monumentally bad parents, refusing to raise kids with values or respect?

But the more I fumed, the more I realized that, ultimately, I was angry at neither the offending kids nor their parents. When I tracked the trail of my anger to its source, I finally identified the person with whom I was upset. Much to my surprise, it was . . . me!

I am a Christian, a follower of Jesus, who calls me to love as he loves. But rather than greeting these three with patience, I was sarcastic and rude. Instead of reaching out to potential new friends or simply asking their names, I pushed them away, content to see three young boys as *them*. Everything I said, and the manner in which I said it, was absolutely in conflict with the person I believe Christ intends me to be. I had poorly represented my church, my faith, and myself. Those kids were probably mumbling that very minute, "No way I'm ever going to that church!"

When we are not what we are meant to be, a clanging rings in our ears, setting our teeth on edge. A dissonance exists. The manner in which Jesus calls us to love and the way in which we act are not in harmony. Our belief and our behavior are out of tune.

Loving only inside the lines may be safe, but it has an unintended effect. The very lines we draw not only shut out others, but they also keep Jesus out. Drawing lines also puts boundaries around joy.

The Samaritan woman was no further beyond the boundaries than you or I, for if not for God's grace, all of us would be outside the lines. When we come to see those around us not as one of *them* but as someone whom Jesus adores, someone for whom he died and in whom he lives, then "they" become "we." Joy returns because our family is whole. We are able to love Jesus in a tangible fashion because we can love him as he comes to us in others.

It is natural to be moved to compassion for those victimized by floods, ravaged by hunger, devastated by natural disasters. Their needs are severe, and we want to help. Christ calls us to help. But these people are usually distant, and we will never cross their paths. They will probably always be nameless faces on the news.

Beyond the random times we send money to alleviate

human suffering—or the unexpected moment we may be called to perilous action—it is in the common moments of a routine life that love comes alive. It is those whose names we know—whose faces populate our community or our offices, who hover on the horizon of our attention—who are our "Canaanite woman."

In loving beyond boundaries and expectations, we experience at a more profound level the depth of Jesus' love for us. In loving outside the lines, we find ordinary joy.

Some Things to Think About

1. How were you raised to draw lines? Who did your family see as "different"?

2. Have you ever been excluded or seen as "different"? How did you feel?

3. What kinds of things cause you to feel outside the circle of Jesus' love? How has Jesus' love made you feel more acceptable?

4. In what ways does your life demonstrate the principle that, in Christ, everyone is welcome, everyone is "in"? How does your church demonstrate that principle?

5. Is there anyone in your life with whom you are out of harmony? What lines have you intentionally, or unintentionally, drawn? Can you think of anyone who would not be welcome in your life or in the life of your congregation?

6. Consider how Jesus might be calling you to reach beyond these boundaries.

chapter twenty

A Final Thought

Then [Jesus] turned toward the woman and said to Simon, "Do you see this woman? . . . I tell you, her many sins have been forgiven—for she loved much."

. . . Jesus said to the woman, "Your faith has saved you; go in peace." (Luke 7:44, 47, 50)

Perhaps the most difficult hurdle to ordinary joy is a sense of dissatisfaction with ourselves and the depth of our faith. We spend a great deal of energy trying to compensate for our ordinariness before others and before God. What it all boils down to is this: Celebrating the ordinary can only happen when we recognize the ordinary as worth celebrating.

My kids and I enjoy spending time together, and I admit taking pleasure in teasing them. So, when my daughter Lisa was younger and would ask me to do something with her, I had a favorite response at the ready.

"Dad, how about a game of cards?" she would ask, already preparing to deal.

"No," I'd mumble, "I really don't feel like playing cards just now."

Lisa then tried another route for motivating her lazy father. "Well, how about some other game?"

"Oh, I don't know."

By then Lisa would be desperate. "Dad, can't we do something?"

The trap was sprung. "Okay," I'd say, "I've got it. Let's pretend. Let's pretend that you're a girl named Lisa and I'm your dad, and you're trying to convince me to do something with you. Don't you think that sounds like a good idea?"

"D-a-a-d," Lisa howled. "That's a dumb idea. I don't want to do that. That's boring. That's what we're doing right now. I want to pretend something else!"

Lisa was less than pleased when I suggested this game because she didn't want to pretend reality; she wanted to pretend fantasy. She wanted to spend time being someone other than who she was, doing something far more exciting. Her problem, though, was that her dad kept suggesting that we "pretend" what was really happening. That was no fun.

We, too, sometimes want to be someone other than who we are. Most of us are well acquainted with what it is like to feel dissatisfied with ourselves. Dissatisfied with our success or lack of it. Dissatisfied in our relationship with God. Dissatisfied with life and faith as it is, thinking it somehow ought to be more pleasing. When we're feeling less than completely content with ourselves and our lives, we'd like to pretend something better. We may work hard, trying lots of different solutions, to conceal what the mirror rudely declares each morning is reality. But that's not the only thing disguised. Carefully hidden away is that part of ourselves that we'd be embarrassed if others knew.

It is difficult to face the deepest, most real version of who we are, much less present that person to the world. It's much easier to pretend that we are satisfied to sample a bland taste of happiness that never quite seems to contain the robust flavor of joy.

Similar to the way that we play "let's pretend" with the world, we are tempted to do the same with God. We offer what we think God wants; we try to be the person we assume God is looking for; we hold back our most real, truest self. We know that God loves us; we proclaim it, we believe it. But we live as if something entirely different is true, as if our achievements affect God's attitude toward us. That is why ordinary faith can seem so dull and unimportant. For all the emphasis on grace, we still try to base our relationship with God on performance.

We think we have to do great things for God, that the ordinary doesn't count. Or it doesn't count for much. The real me does not sufficiently dazzle. The real me does not feel like a good enough parent or spouse, a good enough Christian—often not a good enough person. The real me never quite seems to be sufficient.

So let's pretend, God. Let's pretend that soon I will do something more impressive than the passé things I've done with my faith to this point. I'll pray more. I'll give more. I'll live my faith more fully than I have. Let's pretend, God, that my sin is really just a series of unfortunate mistakes made by someone who is really better than that. Let's pretend, God, that if I shade the truth from you about how I really feel, you'll be less disappointed in me.

We have a God, however, who says, "That's a dumb idea. Let's not pretend. Let's live and celebrate the real thing."

You're not sure? Just ask a woman whose story is told in Luke 7.

She is not remembered for her achievements or her fame. She possessed neither power nor authority. We have no name by which to call her. Luke says nothing of her other than that she was considered to be a person living a sinful life. A disreputable character. Someone with whom no self-respecting person would catch themselves. That, and one thing more.

She crashed a Pharisee's dinner party.

She was an uninvited guest at Simon's soirée. She clearly did not belong in this crowd of proper people where conversation was polite and manners were observed. Slipping in quietly so as to create as little stir as possible, she moved toward the One she had come to see. Awkwardly, she attempted to reach out to Jesus. She mumbled something, and then she was at his feet, crying. Having nothing else to use, she began to dry Jesus' tear-soaked feet with her hair, after which she poured perfume on them.

When Simon, finally at the limit of his tolerance, stood up to take exception to such brazen behavior, Jesus defended her. He noted that her action was rooted in love, growing from the soil of his forgiveness. Then Jesus spoke directly to her, pronouncing forgiveness and commending her faith. From there, she recedes from the pages of Scripture. We don't encounter her again.

What is the key to this woman's action? She gave Jesus the real person she was. She made no attempt to do a great thing for God. She doesn't appear before or after this event healing, preaching, or becoming a martyr for her faith. She simply came to a party one night, dragging her sinful life with her, and wept at Jesus' feet. What she did neither produced nor accomplished anything tangible. It was simply an act in which she gave all of her real self—nothing more or less, nothing hidden or faked, nothing put on—to her Lord.

She did for Jesus what Simon the Pharisee could not. She gave Jesus her honest tears, her matted hair, her real heart. In the giving she discovered what we have difficulty realizing: Covering up is a waste of time because Jesus doesn't condemn. Pretending to be someone we're not, out of a need to be someone more than we are, is a losing game. When this woman met Jesus, he simply said, without looking into her past, wondering about her motives, or inquiring into her intentions, "You are forgiven. You count. Go in peace." He accepted her love at face value and loved her exactly as she was.

It reminds me of a wedding invitation I received some years ago. The invitation said the wedding was informal. As I met with the couple for their pre-marriage work, the prospective bride explained that the event would be outdoors in a friend's backyard and that Barbie and I should dress comfortably and casually.

I took her at her word. It sounded to me like a "come as you are" party.

On the day of the wedding, Barbie and I drove through the neighborhood on our way to the house where I would perform the service. Things didn't look good right from the start. The house turned out to be nestled in the hills of Palos Verde, a tony suburb of Los Angeles, which meant I was stepping into a whole different world than what I was used to.

Pulling up in front of the house, dressed in my Dockers and a button-down shirt, I spotted one of the guests walking across the front yard . . . in a suit. Another couple approached the house from the opposite direction, she in a designer dress and he in a very expensive . . . suit. Barbie and I sat there for a moment watching a parade of people making their way to the backyard, each dressed like they were walking the red carpet at the Academy Awards.

We looked out the window; we glanced down at our totally inadequate outfits; we watched more people arrive; we examined each other's clothes. There was no way we were going to get out of that car dressed in what we were wearing. There was only one thing to do.

As a well-prepared pastor and his wife, we both had brought along more formal clothes just in case we needed them. Barbie crawled into the back seat while I stayed in the front, and we changed clothes. As I tried to wrangle my legs out of my pants and into different ones without throwing the stick shift into neutral or honking the horn, Barbie struggled to get into a dress while hunched down between the seats. All the while, I was desperately hoping—no, I was testing the limits of prayer—that no one would choose that particular moment to walk too close to the car window on their way into the wedding.

A few minutes later we tumbled out of the car, sporting a few wrinkles and with a little adjusting to do, transformed from comfortable and casual to formal and acceptable. Clearly "informal" meant something different to me than it did to everyone else. And that is the worst thing about invitations like that: You're never sure if you should come just as you are, just as you are not, or just as you should be.

Mark this down. Plant it deep in your heart. God's invitation to you is to come as you are, not as you aren't. God is not pleased with you because you are remarkable; you are remarkable because God is pleased with you. Bring your tired, weary, unspectacular self over to Jesus' spot at the table, with little to offer but a sigh or a heart full of hurt, and there you will meet a friend whose glad and tender acceptance sets you free from having to be anything other than who you are. Even when he is poking and probing in the messiest part of a well-hidden heart, Jesus is never offended at our ordinariness. Nor does he demand to know why our response to him has not been more significant. He simply accepts and loves us. Period.

As I sit before the computer screen, struggling to finish this final chapter, I realize how often I have set this project aside, convinced that what I had to say and how I said it would have little value to others. I felt that if the thoughts weren't brilliant or the language didn't crackle, if it didn't stand as a monument to fine writing, it wouldn't be enough. Its value would be suspect. Once again I would turn the computer off, leaving this book to dwell somewhere in the back corner of a hard drive because I feared it would be nothing but ordinary.

I was right. This book isn't a monument. It's not a classic in Christian literature. But I have discovered something in the process. It has been worth writing regardless of how it will be received by publishers or readers, for it has put me in touch with my Lord. And that is enough. It is enough for me because it is enough for Jesus. That is the secret to valuing the ordinary, the key to ordinary joy.

As we struggle with the inadequacy of our discipleship, we are acceptable to Jesus. As we live with the reality of our weak response to this One who has loved us more than life, we are acceptable to him. As we grapple with the disappointments that come attached to ordinary days, we are acceptable to him. When our temper flares at a time it shouldn't, when we snap when we should have loved, when we hoard when we should have given, we are acceptable to him. Nothing we can do will make us more acceptable; nothing we don't do will make us less.

What do you see when you look in the mirror? I hope you see an ordinary person, involved in ordinary living, who is loved by God. That makes you remarkable. I hope you see a person in whom God is well pleased. That makes you noteworthy. I hope the person looking back at you knows that, though your days are filled with the routine and your faith may be unspectacular, God cherishes you. In a delightful twist, which seems to be the hallmark for the way God does things, the very fact that God treasures you just as you are allows your spirit to soar and encourages you to offer your very best to him.

"Let's pretend" might be a great game as a child, but it's an unnecessary one with God. Like the woman at Simon's party, you need hide nothing. Her life began the day she met Jesus whose love received her without question. The grace that touched her heart can put you in touch with the joy that resides in your life. Jesus removes any need to ever pretend before God again.

You are probably pretty ordinary. So am I. But we have an extraordinary Savior. He inhabits the most common moments of life and delights in everyday discipleship, for he rejoices in the ordinary. He rejoices in me, in you.

There is no better reason for joy.

Some Things to Think About

1. In your church, community, or workplace, what pressures do you feel to be someone other than who you are? How do you respond to those pressures?

2. What are some of the ways that you play "Let's pretend" with God?

3. What risk do you think the woman took in coming to Jesus as she did? Can you imagine coming to Jesus with that kind of abandon? What do you think keeps you from coming to Jesus just as you are?

4. Is there someone in your life who accepts you for who you are, someone with whom you do not have to pretend? How does that relationship give you joy?

5. What insight into joy has been most significant for you in reading this book?

About the Author

Joe Campeau is an ordinary guy who happens to be a pastor and is joyful at having been blessed with a wonderful wife, great kids, and the love of an extraordinary God. He thinks living and serving with the people of Christ Lutheran Church in Santa Clarita, California, is a great adventure. He's also interested in hearing your story of God's presence in your life. You can reach him at pastorjoe@sbcglobal.net.

Other Resources from Augsburg

Morning B.R.E.W. by Kirk Byron Jones
128 pages, 0-8066-5138-5

Unlike other morning devotions, in which you digest the
words of others, this book teaches you how to create your
own devotional experiences through silence and prayerful
visualization.

Morning B.R.E.W. Journal by Kirk Byron Jones
112 pages, 0-8066-5143-1

Filled with encouraging quotes and inspirational thoughts to
"jump-start" a B.R.E.W. experience, the journal provides a
place for people to record and reflect on memorable B.R.E.W.
experiences.

Step Up by Richard C. Meyer
160 pages, 0-8066-5135-0

Meyer has creatively re-purposed the Twelve Steps into a
biblically-based model for change and spiritual renewal. He
shows how the Twelve Steps can be a tool for spiritual healing
for everyone, not just the addicted.

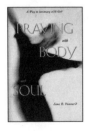

Praying with Body and Soul by Jane E. Vennard
144 pages, 0-8066-3614-9

Praying with Body and Soul involves the whole person. By
paying prayerful attention to the body, people will not only
recognize the ways in which they already pray, but will learn
how to deepen their relationship with God.

Available wherever books are sold.